Florencewalks

ANNE HOLLER

Florencewalks

Photographs by Daniel Bloch

A New Republic Book
Holt, Rinehart and Winston
New York

To my father

First published in February 1983 by Holt, Rinehart and Winston,
383 Madison Avenue, New York, New York 10017.

Published simultaneously in Canada by Holt, Rinehart and Winston of
Canada, Limited.

Library of Congress Cataloging in Publication Data

Holler, Anne.
Florencewalks.
"A New republic book."
Includes index.
1. Florence (Italy)—Description—1981-   —Tours.
I. Title.
DG732.H64   914.5'51   82-1107
                                 AACR2

ISBN Paperback: 0-03-059938-5

First Edition

Designer: Jacqueline Schuman
Printed in the United States of America
1 3 5 7 9 10 8 6 4 2

ISBN 0-03-059938-5

Contents

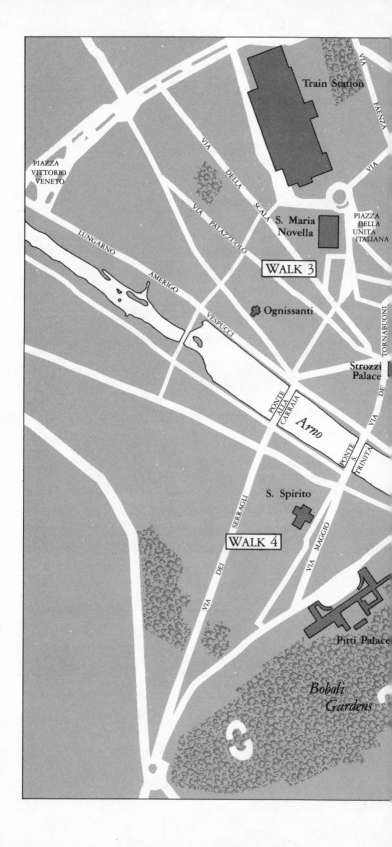

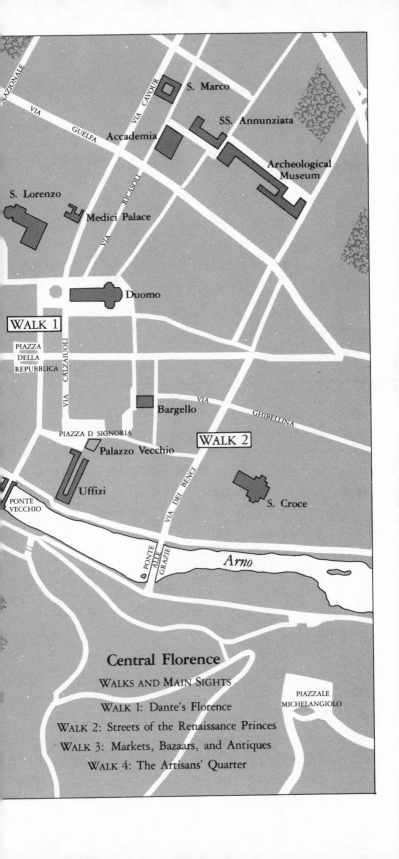

NAZIONALE

VIA
GUELFA

VIA CAVOUR

S. Marco

Accademia

SS. Annunziata

RICASOLI

Archeological
Museum

S. Lorenzo

VIA

Medici Palace

Duomo

WALK 1

VIA CALZAIUOLI

PIAZZA
DELLA
REPUBBLICA

Bargello

VIA
GHIBELLINA

PIAZZA D SIGNORIA

Palazzo Vecchio

WALK 2

Uffizi

VIA DEI BENCI

S. Croce

PONTE
VECCHIO

PONTE
ALLE
GRAZIE

Arno

Central Florence

WALKS AND MAIN SIGHTS

WALK 1: Dante's Florence

WALK 2: Streets of the Renaissance Princes

WALK 3: Markets, Bazaars, and Antiques

WALK 4: The Artisans' Quarter

PIAZZALE
MICHELANGIOLO

Acknowledgments

I would like to thank the many Florentines—along the walks and inside shops, restaurants, banks, churches, and libraries—who have helped me with information, anecdotes, and access to corners of the city seldom seen by the passerby. In particular, I am grateful to Barbara and Bill Larson for always keeping a key under the mat for me, to Catherine and Tim Larson for pointing out to me what children like to do and see in Florence, to Sandra Celli, Polly and Carlo Colella, and to Anna Nathanson.

On the other side of the ocean, I wish to thank Professor Gene Brucker of the University of California at Berkeley and Professor Brenda Preyer of the University of Texas at Austin for their invaluable research suggestions. For starting me off in the right direction I thank Judith Haber, and for help along the way, Charles Kaiser and Bernard Alter.

I'm especially grateful to Marc Granetz, the editor of this book, for suggesting the idea of *Florencewalks* to me and for polishing my often cloudy prose.

Finally, I would like to thank Daniel for his patience, translating abilities, good humor, and for being not only an excellent photographer but also the best traveling companion inside or out of Florence.

Florencewalks

Introduction

A friend of mine once said to me, "Visiting Florence is like calling at your great-aunt's house. You walk around very carefully because you're afraid of knocking over and breaking something precious."

Over the centuries, the image of Florence as precious has developed a patina as polished as a priceless bronze. The Renaissance is heralded as an era of unparalleled achievements in art, architecture, and science, and Florence was the magic city in which these marvels were born. One is supposed to visit Florence with a cultivated eye and with awe for good taste, the fine arts, and ecclesiastical grace.

But in reality Florence is not as delicate or demure as most travel brochures and coffee-table books might lead us to think. The city has a vivid, volatile history—Christian martyrs thrown to lions, neighborhood clans engaged in bloody vendettas in the streets, poorly paid wool-workers rioting in the marketplaces until their voices were heard in the powerful guild halls.

Florence is a dollhouse setting for much of the theater of Italian social history—in fact, for much of the social history of the Western World. In the first two centuries before Christ, Florence (or Florentia) was little more than a factory town and Roman port. Iron making was probably the chief industry. Ore that was extracted on the island of Elba and shipped up to Pisa was brought down along the wide stretch of the Arno to Florentia.

Overlooking the port and its activities was the Etruscan town of Fiesole. The Etruscans were a proud group of people who traced their ancestors back to Asian nomads and Sandon, the king of Babylonia. When and how they settled in Italy are unresolved matters, but at some time a delegation from southern Lydia in Asia Minor may have been responsible for introducing Greek art and culture into their lives. Depictions of Hercules, equipped with his bow and metal mace, have been found in Etruscan tombs, and his lion is still part of the emblem of Florence today.

Fiesole was captured by Roman armies in the second century B.C. Three concentric walls were built around the hilltop, and a fourth wall extended down to Florentia and the Arno. The entrances to this enormous citadel were along the river's edge. Three gates, spaced a mile apart, were the only access to the occupied town. The Roman general Sulla parceled out tracts of Florentia to members of his twenty-three legions. The soldiers, in turn, showed their allegiance to the mother city, Rome, by building a miniature copy complete with a Field of Mars, a Forum, a Temple of Mars, baths, a theater, an amphitheater, and an aqueduct.

Fiesole, meanwhile, played a very different role. The town became the center of soothsaying in the Roman world. Long known for its skilled body of priests trained in the rites of sacrifice and divination, Fiesole annually welcomed twelve Roman youths who were sent to the hillside temples to study augury. In the first century A.D., Pliny remembers the auspicious sight of a Fiesolan entering the gates of Rome accompanied by his seventy-four sons and grandsons and a commission to carry out some serious soothsaying.

In the same century, Christian converts began to invade Florentia. The Christians were persecuted—thrown to lions in the amphitheater—on and off throughout the third century A.D. But by 313 a bishop was living safely in Florence; it's likely that the first Christian cathedral was built around this time too. The Church of San Salvador was the name of the edifice, and its location was quite near if not directly under what is now the Cathedral of Santa Maria del Fiore in the Piazza del Duomo. Sandwiched between the first cathedral and the last was Santa Reparata, a church named for a twelve-year-old female martyr. The young saint was said to have appeared in the middle of a fifth-century battle between a host of Vandals and Goths and the citizens of Fiesole. Santa Reparata suddenly arrived on the spot with a bloodred banner and a lily in her hand. Miraculously, following close behind her was the Roman general Stilicho with a fresh legion of troops. The barbarians fought a losing battle, and the Florentines built a new cathedral in remembrance of the girl's military assistance.

Money-making, church-building, and nobility-feuding were the activities of primary importance in the

newly cosmopolitan Florence of the thirteenth century. Frescoes, paintings, statues, murals, and tapestries
were the artistic accessories to a world that was wak-
ing up to self-expression, creativity, vanity, material-
ism, and physical adornment.

Art masterpieces and Florence are synonymous. On
my twenty-first birthday I made my first pilgrimage to
the shrines of Michelangelo, Brunelleschi, Ghiberti,
and Giotto. As an art student, I spent the obligatory
hours in the Uffizi Gallery, the Pitti Palace, the Convent of San Marco, and the Accademia delle Belle Arti.
Over the years, as I've visited family and friends in
Florence with new personal interest in archaeology,
urban planning, and architecture, I have continually
seen the city from new perspectives. I have come to
understand how the great artworks, the churches, the
palaces, the commercial life, and the very shape and
pattern of the city were all products of an extraordi-
nary group of men and women who have lived and
earned a living here.

The four walks in this book were chosen with this
large perspective in mind. After strolling around the
streets of Florence your impression of the town and its
masterpieces may change greatly. You may begin to
reflect on the history of this unique city and of the
people—Christian saints and martyrs, Saxon princes,
French usurpers, English expatriates—who have
flocked here. The first walk centers on the very core of
Florence's history: the Old Market, guild halls, medieval towers, and crooked alleyways where Dante used
to roam. Some of the highlights of the second walk—a
doll hospital, the site of the ancient lions' dens, a top-
notch ice-cream salon, some fishermen and perhaps a
boat race on the Arno—make it (even in an abbreviated form) especially appealing to children. The third
walk winds around thirteenth- and fourteenth-century
buildings, open-air markets, and elegant, inviting
shops of all varieties. The fourth walk on the other
bank of the Arno takes in the oldest woodworking district in Florence, some famous frescoes that Leonardo
da Vinci, Raphael, and Michelangelo used to study,
and one of the few streets in the city that still looks exactly as it did at the height of the Renaissance.

Florence is not Paris, London, or Rome. It's an over-
grown village with rival churches and monastic orders,

marble gods and goddesses, and four-hundred-year-old palaces at every turn. The town is compact; almost any point can be reached with a little determination and a bit of time. Visitors usually come to Florence with a curiosity about and a lot of interest in history, art, architecture, and Italian life. I hope *Florencewalks* will speak to those interests, and enhance every visitor's experience of this remarkable city.

Information and Advice

Before You Go

Any trip you're planning—to the next town or to a foreign port halfway around the world—will be more enjoyable if you do a little homework ahead of time. When it concerns Florence, the reward for such diligence is calm nerves. One of the most frequent complaints about Florence is that museums and virtually every store in town shut down at 1:00 or 2:00 in the afternoon for an unhurried lunch hour. The museums do not reopen until the following day; most of the stores will unlock their doors around 3:30 or 4:00. The smaller the store the less precise will be the hour of reopening. Often a proprietor will hang a cardboard, handwritten sign on his or her front door that gives an approximate time of return. Don't take the time too literally. There's always a leeway of about a half hour. The point here is that you should *plan ahead* if you want to take in galleries, museums, some shopping, and (I hope) a few walking tours on a tight schedule.

You'll want to enjoy leisurely hours in the art-filled galleries of the Uffizi Palace, the Pitti Palace, the Bargello, the Palazzo Vecchio, and the Accademia delle Belle Arti where Michelangelo's *David* is housed; and no trip to Florence would be complete without a visit to the famous churches that are themselves architectural works of art: the Cathedral of Santa Maria del Fiore ("the Duomo"), the Baptistery, Santa Croce with the celebrated Giotto frescoes, Santa Maria Novella where Michelangelo worked as an apprentice to Ghirlandaio, San Lorenzo and the Medici Chapels, and the convent of San Marco decorated with Fra Angelico's delicate paintings.

The more practical information you accumulate and think over beforehand, the happier you'll be about how you spend your time in Florence. Write to or call the Italian Government Travel Office at any of the following locations several weeks in advance of your trip:

630 Fifth Avenue
New York, New York 10020
212-245-4822

500 North Michigan Avenue
Chicago, Illinois 60611
312-644-0990

360 Post Street
San Francisco, California 94018
415-392-6206

Ask for all their information on Florence (plus any oth-er Italian cities you plan to visit). You'll receive a travel packet of sights-to-see, the hours of opening, a list of hotels and restaurants, and a map of the city.

You'll be welcome to stay in Florence or anywhere else in Italy for three months with a valid American passport. If you think that you may want to stay lon-ger, apply for a visa *before* you leave. (Contact any Ital-ian consulate in the United States.) Visas are not always granted easily once you are inside the Italian border.

The summer months in Florence are warm, if not semitropical at times. June is hard to predict. The last few years have seen cooler-than-normal temperatures for this month, so you may want to pack more than the obligatory sweater if you'll be visiting then. A light-weight raincoat, sunglasses, and comfortable shoes are the right accessories for an Italian summer. Winters are very rainy, and occasionally snowy, cold, and damp. Heating systems in even the most elegant establish-ments are temperamental. Long underwear, plenty of wool socks, and a few layers of sweaters should see you through a less hectic but chillier tourist season. Al-though Florence has some of the most fashion-con-scious citizens in the world, you'll still be well received in the fanciest restaurants in a simple skirt and blouse or trousers and a sports jacket. Members of the nobili-ty are dressing down these days to fend off unwarrant-ed attention; you too can be mistaken for a countess, a duke, or a Milanese television magnate in a simple pair of jeans (and minus your jewel collection). When you visit churches and galleries, don't wear anything out-landish or designed especially for the beach unless you want to attract a lot of stares. Woman wearing short skirts or women or men wearing "unconserva-tive" clothing are occasionally refused entry to churches.

Try to read as much about Florence, its history, art, and architecture, as you are able before setting out on your trip. Browse through books on the painters and sculptors whose works you'll see in Florence. If there's one artist who particularly interests you, make yourself knowledgeable about his work. When you're actually standing in front of his canvas or statue in a Florentine gallery or chapel, you'll truly appreciate your scholarly efforts.

The following is a suggested, highly abbreviated reading list of works that will suffuse you with Italian culture while you're still in the armchair stage of your travels.

John Ciardi's translation of Dante's *Divina Comme-dia* (*The Divine Comedy*) is a clear, informative inter-pretation of the cornerstone of Italian literature and the first classic work written in the Italian vernacular that is still used today. Iris Origo's historical account of the millionaire but miserly *Merchant of Prato* is based on the life of the fourteenth-century textile trader Francesco di Marco Datini. Origo, a noted Renaissance scholar, went through five hundred ledgers and thou-sands of letters left behind by this Italian Horatio Al-ger. This is a little-recognized and highly readable record of Renaissance daily life right down to the smallest domestic details. (The reader will learn that Renaissance men and women seldom wore night-clothes but always donned little nightcaps!) Jacob Burckhardt's *The Civilization of the Renaissance in Italy* (1860) is a scholarly survey by one of the fore-most writers about the period. For a contemporary look at Florence's art colony life during the Renais-sance, read Vasari's *Lives of the Artists*. Just as enter-taining and slightly more worthy of being "X-rated" is the *Autobiography* of sixteenth-century goldsmith and sculptor Benvenuto Cellini. Memories of his amatory and homicidal adventures may have a more lasting ef-fect on your imagination than his sculptural master-pieces in Florence's Bargello Museum.

For much lighter reading, dip into Irving Stone's well-researched fictional account of Michelangelo's life, *The Agony and the Ecstasy*. An extensive bibliography, a glossary of Italian words and phrases, and a listing of where Michelangelo's works are to be found is included at the end. *A Room with a View* by E. M. Forster takes a lingering look at Florence through the slightly hazy eyes of a nineteenth-century English maiden, Lucy Honeychurch, as she daringly walks—without a chaperone—through the town under the spell of newly awakened feelings of love. Mary McCarthy's *Stones of Florence* is an irreverent twentieth-century look at the cradle of the Renaissance. Her critique of Michelangelo's "rubbery" statues in the Medici Chapel still raises the dander of all Florentines and art lovers.

For a juicy look at the life of international art connoisseur and indefatigable ladies' man Bernard Berenson, read Meryle Secrest's biography, *Being Bernard Berenson*.

General Information

If you arrive in Florence by way of the train station, the best first move you could make is to leave it quickly behind. Avoid cashing money and asking for information here because the lines are long and you'll only fray your nerves within the first half hour of your visit. Under no circumstances should you consider buying an international train ticket for the next leg of your trip at the station. The Italian system of waiting in three different (and often long) lines—for a reservation, an overnight berth, and a train ticket, respectively—is a test of patience no one should voluntarily undergo. For all information and travel reservations go directly to American Express. If this sounds small-minded and chauvinistic, you'll be happy for once that you were. There are two branches of American Express in Florence. The bank is at via della Vigna Nuova 8/r; it's closed on Saturdays and Sundays. All other services (mail, traveler's checks, travel information, and reservations) are in the smaller office called "Universaltourismo" at via degli Speziali 7/r, right off the Piazza della Repubblica in the center of Florence. It's open Monday through Friday, 9:00 A.M. to 12:30 P.M. and 3:00 to 7:00 P.M.; on Saturdays, 9:30 A.M. to 12:00 noon; and it's closed on Sundays (tel. 217.241). If you're a student and you want help with budget travel and accommodations, walk over to Student Travel (CGTS) at via delle Terme 53/r, which is just off Piazza Santa Trinità. They're open Monday through Friday from 9:00 A.M. to 12:30 P.M. and 3:00 to 6:00 P.M. and closed Saturday afternoons and all day Sunday (tel. 292.150).

In your travels around Florence, you'll notice that the street numbers are written in either black or red. Black numbers indicate residential buildings; red indicates commercial establishments such as stores, restaurants, and hotels. Whenever an address is followed by the letter *r* (for red), you'll know that the building is a place of business. To add to the confusion, the numbers of both colors do not correspond in any way to each other. A no. 3 (black) may be next door to a no. 37/r (red), so don't expect much logic when you're looking for an address. At least Florence is a small town, so you won't have to wander too far to find the right address.

Most Florentines, especially those who come into daily contact with visitors, do speak English. If you find yourself in a situation where this is not the case, don't be afraid to try and communicate with a mixture of Italian and English or even a dash of French, which is sometimes close enough. Remember that Florentines are cosmopolitan and they're used to speaking with non-Italians. Many merchants are quick to help a foreigner understand prices or bills for thousands of lire. They'll itemize or write your total bill down on a piece of paper if you really need to have that done.

For local excursions around Florence, drop in at the main office of the Compagnia Italiana Turismo (CIT), via de' Cerretani 57–59/r, near the center of Florence (tel. 294.306). This organization offers three-and-a-half-hour tours of the standard Florentine sights in the convenience of a modern air-conditioned bus. There's a morning tour and an afternoon tour. Theater and concert tickets can be purchased here also.

Tickets and information for plays and musical events can be procured also at the box offices of three of Florence's best-known theaters. Teatro Niccolini is at via Ricasoli 3; plays and concerts are held several times a week in this sumptuous seventeenth-century hall. A smaller, intimate theater with a wide selection of dramatic events is the Teatro dell'Oriuolo at via dell'Oriuolo 31. Across the Arno, at Borgo San Jacopo 36, is the more experimental theater group Teatro il Punto; their productions are often held in the open piazzas and cloisters of neighborhood medieval churches. Most of the theatrical events in Florence will be in Italian but any lack of understanding the language should not keep you away from the entertainment.

During the summer months Florence plays host to classical musicians, jazz ensembles, opera singers, country and western groups, and hard-rock bands. The famous music festival Maggio Musicale Fiorentino leans more toward the classical and is held during May and June. Most of the summer musical entertainment is held under the stars, in the open piazzas facing the grand Renaissance churches, and it's free. In December, movie buffs from all over Europe head for Florence's Festival of Documentary Films. The nearby Etruscan town of Fiesole also beckons to cultural enthusiasts while putting its Roman amphitheater to good use. Jazz and classical concerts are presented throughout the summer in this unmatched classical setting. Keep your eyes open for posters displayed on Florence's street corners: posters are the main source of communication for most of the entertainment offerings in the city. If some upcoming event interests you, jot down the time and place because the chances are slim that you will see the information printed elsewhere.

Movie listings are advertised in Florence's newspaper, *La Nazione*. (One movie theater, the Astro Cinema in Piazza San Simone, offers English and American films exclusively, but the management seems to take extended vacations during the summer months.) Other papers that are avidly read by the local citizens are the *Corriere della Sera* from Milan and *La Città*, which is fairly easy reading for the elementary student in Italian. English-reading visitors are always assured of the availability of the *International Herald Tribune* and another journal with less of a "hard news" approach, the *Daily American*. Founded in 1945, this paper is published and printed in Rome. If you're particularly homesick for the sight of the English language or in the mood for some light conversational news stories, then by all means buy it. These papers are sold in the many newsstands around the train station.

Swimming facilities in and around Florence can be crowded, so brace yourself for a lot of company if you venture out to the pools. Children will enjoy the playgrounds and swimming at Campo di Marte (take bus number 17 from the train station). Bus A also leaves from the station and goes to the Piscina le Pavoniere. Both pools are open from 10:00 A.M. until 7:00 P.M. throughout the summer. The admission charge is L1,500.

Accommodations

Make hotel reservations several months in advance. The Italian mail service is legendary for the slowness of its service, and it is entirely possible that your letter requesting a room will arrive in Florence many weeks after you do. The best insurance against hotel reservation problems is to make them through your travel agent.

To enjoy Florence in the "grand manner" you may want to consider staying at any of the following. The Grand Hotel Minerva, near the center of town, is an elegant establishment that overlooks Piazza Santa Maria Novella and the regal church of the same name. The Grand Hotel Majestic is located in the quiet via del Melarancio ("Street of the Pomegranate"). The Savoy is everything its name implies; it reigns over what once was the Roman Forum and medieval marketplace of Florence and is now Piazza della Repubblica. The Excelsior Italie is the last word in Florentine taste. This hotel, with a sweeping view of the Arno, started out in 1480 as the Palazzo Ricasoli. Much of the interior marble inlay work and carving was added in the sixteenth century. In the nineteenth century, this sumptuous residence turned into the Hotel New-York. Old photographs of this era show a stream of horse-and-buggies flowing down the boulevard along the Arno and around the Hotel New-York. Today, the Excelsior Italie is more likely to be the scene of dark-glassed limousines parked around the Piazza Goldoni and in front of the main entrance. On the other side of the Arno is the sleek and modern lungarno in Borgo San Jacopo. Built after the last war, this hotel has an unmatched view of the Arno, the fourteenth-century Ponte Vecchio, and the modest skyline of old Florence.

There are any number of moderately-priced, attractive hotels. A few possibilities that are near the center of Florence and the walks in this book are: Della Signoria in via delle Terme, Hotel City in via Sant' Antonino, Berchielli on lungarno Acciaiuoli, and Porta Rossa in via Porta Rossa. A quiet and charming hotel, Monna Lisa, is housed in a Renaissance palace along the old medieval street of Borgo Pinti. There are five comfortable living rooms to relax or entertain in, a flower-bedecked garden in the courtyard, and a resident "contessa" who is straight out of an Auntie Mame novel. On another literary note, you may want to stay at the relatively inexpensive Pensione Bartolini on lungarno Guicciardini. This is where E. M. Forster's characters sojourned in *A Room with a View* while they toured the town. Also on the economical side is the Hotel Santa Croce in via Bentaccordi. This lodging is popular with visiting art students and professors.

Across the river in the Oltr'arno are two pleasant hotels with modest rates: La Scaletta in via Guicciardini and, in Piazza Santo Spirito, the Pensione Bandini, another Renaissance-palace-turned-hotel.

Check with your travel agent about price ranges and special services or write to the Italian Government Travel Office (see pages 5–6) for complete and up-to-date brochures on hotels.

Transportation

Walking is the sanest way to get around Florence. Driving is hazardous to your health—mental and physical—and there's no real reason to take to the wheel unless you are entering or leaving the city. If you find yourself in either situation, you should be forewarned that many intersections away from the center of the city are ambiguously managed by both pedestrians and motorists. Many corners have neither stop signs nor traffic lights, and there's a continuous game of Russian roulette to see who is going to get through the impasse without coming out looking like an accordion. Over the decades, Florentines have developed a sixth sense for surviving and even enjoying this test of intuition, endurance, and timing. If you're a pedestrian at one of these intersections, it's often best to stand back and wait for the flow of vehicles to go through their maneuvers before attempting to cross. Despite the seeming abundance of cars around Florence, this method of transportation is still a great luxury. Garages are expensive, gasoline is almost $4 a gallon these days, and mechanical service is virtually on a par with the cost of medical care. Motorcycles and motorscooters are also relatively expensive ways of getting around Florence but they are easier to handle and park than cars. Bicycles and walking, for many Florentines, are still the cheapest and sometimes fastest ways to travel over bridges, through narrow stone-paved streets, and around traffic-clogged piazzas. Walking, for the unitiated, is the safest and, in many ways, the most pleasant way to get around the town.

Almost any bus you may want to take in Florence passes through and stops in front of the Duomo, the Cathedral of Santa Maria del Fiore. If you're going to the nearby town of Fiesole, look for the number 7 bus, which also stops in Piazza San Marco. Bus tickets are bought in bar-cafés or tobacco (*tabacchi*) stores. For the last decade buses in Florence have been running on the honor system. Passengers enter the vehicle from the back door and insert their tickets in a machine that stamps them with the date and time. You'll see plenty of Florentines "forgetting" to follow this procedure. The city is now beginning to realize that it's losing money on this system and more and more bus inspectors are popping on board to check tickets.

Taxi stands are set up at most of the larger piazzas around Florence. Many of the drivers congregate either at the train station or in front of the Duomo. Yellow cabs are the official city taxis to use. A new law has just gone into effect: all rides, regardless of how short, begin with a L2,000 minimum. A 15 percent tip is customary. To telephone for taxi service, call 4798.

If you want to take an out-of-town bus ride—for example, to Siena or San Gimignano—walk over to the SITA station, which is around the corner from the train station at via Santa Caterina di Siena 15/r. The telephone number is 294.647. These buses leave the station according to the schedule with astonishing precision. Be sure that you allow plenty of time to locate your bus and board at leisure.

Food and Drink

After the great works of art and architecture in Florence, the visitor to this city cannot help but be impressed by its refreshments. Northern Italian cooking (unlike a rival foreign cuisine) is low on heavy sauces, creams, and elaborate liqueur embellishments. It's high on simple but exquisitely prepared dishes. Every slice of fresh meat or ripe vegetable is cooked to bring out its best natural taste, not to drown or smother the dish with high-calorie or alien concoctions. Meals in even the snazziest restaurants are still prepared as if one were invited to a feast at the long trestle table of a prosperous and well-stocked farm.

If you appreciate a good steak, you're in the right town. Florence is famous for its *bistecca alla fiorentine*. The beef cattle around Florence in the Tuscan hills are raised on a carefully grown diet of rich grasses, and the result of this effort is a memorable cut of sweet, tender meat. While you're here you may also want to try *lepre* (hare), *cinghiale* (wild boar), the always popular *coniglio* (rabbit), and *finocchiona* (a fennel-flavored sausage). Fennel has been the official herb of Florence for centuries. Dedicated to the patron saint of the city, John the Baptist, fennel was given to invalids for strength and to underweight people for extra poundage. Mixed with honey, fennel is guaranteed to cure bites from hungry mad dogs. You'll also see on some Florentine menus a dish called *cibreo*. Literally translated it means a "medley" or "muddle." Culinarily translated it means a fricassee of eggs and giblets. Another classic Florentine treat is *trippa* (tripe), and it can be had for a lot of money or a little. Some restaurants produce a delicate, marinated tripe dish served as an elegant antipasto. Cooked tripe arranged on a slice of bread is also sold in outdoor stands (*trippaioli*) in the working-class section of Borgo San Frediano and in Piazza Alighieri just off via dei Cerchi.

Seafood in Florentine restaurants is often delicious

(and as expensive as meat), but it is by no means a local specialty. Most of the fish dishes, such as squid, octopus, and lobster, were caught in the northern waters of the Tyrrhenian Sea and then frozen for the trip down to Florence.

Gardens are a passion for almost every Italian who has access to even a few square yards of earth, and as a result vegetables are treated with respect. Ordinary zucchini, cauliflower, and broccoli are often cooked in garlic and oil, and they emerge from the kitchen tasting like a dish fit for a king. *Fagioli* (white or green beans) are a Florentine favorite and you'll see them as a selection on almost every menu. They're usually boiled and served either hot or cold with oil and vinegar. Bright orange zucchini flowers sold all over the markets are transformed into a delicacy when dipped in a rich batter and deep-fried. An eating establishment that rivals a pizza stand any day is the *frittoria*. Here, not only zucchini flowers but also slices of eggplant, pumpkin, onions, artichokes, peppers, cauliflower, parsnips, and even lettuce are covered with a crisp, deep-fried coating. These days there are fewer *frittorias* around the center of Florence, but you can also find these fried vegetable assortments in the more ubiquitous *rosticceria*. In these casual restaurants you'll find that the focal point is a roaring fireplace in which a rotating spit is studded with plump, roasting chickens. You can order a whole or part of a chicken to take out or eat there if tables and chairs are in evidence. Other side dishes might be *gnocchi di spinaci* ("spinach dumplings") and *bietole bollite e ricotte* ("boiled beets with ricotta cheese").

Fruits during the summer in Italy are unforgettable. There's an unwritten law in the marketplace that the customer does not handle the fruits or vegetables. Tell the merchant how much produce you want, and he or she will do the choosing. Remember that most fruit is sold underripe so that it will be perfect for dinner the next day, or after. Melons are particularly memorable in Florence; they're also a luxury and may cost as much as L2,000 each. If you're going to a dinner party, you'll be just as welcome with a cantaloupe or honeydew under your arm as a bottle of wine.

Many visitors, especially the budget-minded ones, like to remember Florence for its low-priced but excellent wine. A wonderful table or picnic wine can be bought for less than L2,000. Tuscany produces a special rich red wine called Chianti Classico. You'll see several brands with this name on the label, but the official government-approved Classico will always have a black rooster conspicuously displayed on the bottle.

Wine cafés used to be as numerous around Florence as coffee shops are today. Along the walks you'll run into a few of these still-cherished urban oases. The cafés will either be marked *Vini* ("Wines") or *Fiaschetteria* ("Wine Shop"). The former is more of a bar where you can order a glass of red or white wine and drink it near the counter or in the street while gossiping with a group of friends. The latter can be anything from a store selling glasses or bottles of wine to a full-sized restaurant with a large choice of wines to consider enjoying with your meal. If you're not a wine drinker or you prefer a side drink with your wine, most restaurants serve *acqua minerale* ("mineral water") and *acqua gassosa* (an effervescent carbonated water). Beer can be expensive especially if it's imported. Hard liquor, sodas, and tonic water are also slightly more expensive than what you may be used to paying. Plain tap water is safe to drink, although it's a little metallic-tasting. When you're out walking around the town, remember that many of Florence's wall fountains are gushing out fresh spring water that's even better than what comes out of the faucets.

Cheeses, along with wedges of fruit, are considered dessert. *Pecorino*, ("sheep cheese") is usually fresh and in abundance by May or June. A mild, soft cheese similar to Camembert is *stracchino*.

Breads and pastry in Florence vary from store to store. Look for older shops around the Mercato Centrale, and you'll find small fruit tarts and large loaves of bread.

Coffee for coffee-lovers is as special here as wine is for wine-lovers. For most Florentines breakfast is a cup of *caffè*, *caffelatte* (hot milk added), or *cappuccino* (espresso topped off with steamed milk). A small pastry or two may be consumed but not much else. Appetites are being conditioned for the more relaxed and plentiful afternoon dinner hours. This early morning meal is generally shared in a sociable manner at a neighborhood bar-café. The coffee habit is catching on all over Italian cities, and now it's quite normal to see office workers and shop clerks rushing out to a café in mid-morning for a large order of coffees to go. Many restaurants, however, still do not serve coffee at the end of the meal, and if you miss this familiar touch you'll have to search out a bar-café after dessert.

If ice cream is really what you're looking for, try the favorite spots of the Florentines: Perchè No in via de' Tavolini, just off via dei Cerchi (see page 68), and the Gelateria in Piazza Santo Spirito (see pages 155–58). Vivoli's in via dell'Isola delle Stinche (see pages 94–95) is world-famous but patronized more by Americans than any other group.

Tipping

Although hotels and restaurants automatically add a 15 percent service charge to your bill, it's customary to leave an extra tip for helpful personnel and waiters. In hotels, a general guide to follow is: chambermaid, 500–800 lire a day; bellhop, 500 lire per bag; doorman who calls a cab, 300–500 lire; and any valet or room service, at least 500 lire. In restaurants, leave an extra 5–10 percent of your total bill for the waiter. If a wine steward assisted you, a tip of 10 percent of the wine bill can be left. After an espresso or *caffè*, a tip of L100 is usually left at the bar. In some establishments you are still requested to pay the cashier before you order; in that case the L100 tip is usually handed over (with the receipt the cashier gives you) to the person behind the counter.

Telephone, Telegraph, Post Office

Telephone, telegraph, and post office services are available at Florence's Central Post Office in via Pelicceria. The main entrance is directly across from Piazza della Repubblica.

Telephones are to the right of the front door and they are ready for use twenty-four hours a day, seven days a week. International calls are handled through assistants in the phone company here. Keep in mind that although calls to foreign countries are expensive (about L3,000 a minute on weekdays and L2,000 from 11:00 P.M. Sunday to 11:00 A.M. Monday), you'll be charged a lot less at this office than by a hotel operator.

Local calls in Florence are made with the purchase of *gettone*, telephone tokens that cost L100 each. They can be bought at vending machines in the train and bus stations or in any bar. *Gettone* are also given out as change. (Some postal clerks who are short of small change and *gettone* will pay you with little paper-wrapped candies.) In every phone booth there are instructions on how to place a call. You'll be able to talk for five minutes with one token. When you hear beeps, deposit a few more tokens. Push the "return" button after your conversation and any *gettone* that are owed to you will come out of the slot.

Telegrams in Italy cost approximately L500 a word and they are the fastest and most reliable way to get in touch with someone in another country. Your telegram will be wired and delivered the next day.

The postal section of this cavernous building is open from 8:15 A.M. until 7:30 P.M., Monday through Saturday; it's closed on Sunday. Buy your stamps at the counter. Mark all letters and postcards "via aerea" as an extra precaution against the dreaded surface mail, and deposit your letters outside the post office in the red mailboxes against the front wall.

Money and Banking

Banks in Florence are open Monday through Friday from 8:30 A.M. to 1:30 P.M. They're closed all day Saturday and Sunday. If you're cashing traveler's checks, try to get to the bank either very early in the banking day or just before it closes to avoid long lines. Bring your passport—and something to read if you think that you'll be caught in a crowd.

Most major credit cards such as American Express or Visa are accepted in stores, restaurants, and hotels around Florence. Check with a restaurant, however, before arriving for a large meal.

There is a VAT (Value Added Tax) on all goods and services provided in Florence. This means that the merchant has paid the taxes on all raw materials that go into a product. The consumer pays a certain amount of the cost of production when purchasing an item, but there is no extra sales tax added onto the bill for anything that you may buy.

Shopping

The shops in Florence range from the glossy and ultraelegant to the intimate and offbeat. Traditional Florentine wares include fine leather goods, lace and embroidery, gold jewelry, glass, silver and porcelain ornaments, hand-dyed marbleized paper, antiques and excellent reproductions of antiques. The streets of via Maggio, via Tornabuoni, and via della Vigna Nuova are ports of call for shops such as Gucci and Ferragamo and the world-renowned quality that has made Florence famous for fashion and decoration. The city also has a growing number of younger craftspeople who are trying their hands at businesses on a less sophisticated scale. Along the streets of Borgo degli Alfani and Borgo Pinti (near Walk 2) and Piazza Santo Spirito (on Walk 4) there are new shops filled with handcrafted jewelry, pottery, vintage and one-of-a-kind clothes, gallery posters from around the world, and papier-mâché theater masks.

Florence's two popular outdoor markets, the Mercato Nuovo and the stalls around the Mercato Centrale, are stocked with inexpensive items. The Mercato Nuovo is the established straw market of the city, but you'll also find some colorful embroidered linens for sale. A visit to the bazaar near the Mercato Centrale may yield some bargains in old clothes, toys, and more leather and straw merchandise.

A flea market that's not so well known to Florentine visitors but is worth investigating for curious antiques and anonymous artworks is located near the area of Walk 2. At the end of via dell'Oriuolo is via Pietrapiana. Walk about 50 yards down this street; look for the open market, Logge del Pesce, or the Old Fish Market, and on your right in the Piazza Ciompi you'll spot the small buildings of the flea-market merchants. The tiny showrooms and display windows are filled with everything from Art Deco living-room sets to the hand-embroidered cassocks of a country priest. In the summer months, this flea market is open every day except Sunday.

Contrary to lots of rumors, bargaining in the various marketplaces around Florence is not common. Behind the casual storefronts of the stalls around the Mercato Centrale and the Mercato Nuovo are merchants who are professional businessmen. They've waited years for a license and a spot in the markets, and they're legally obliged to appear there every working day for fifteen years. Prices are carefully determined, and it's only occasionally that a merchant agrees to sell two or more of the same items for a discount.

Most of the merchants in the open marketplaces are ready for business by 9:00 in the morning. They close down their stalls around 1:30 or 2:00 in the afternoon and don't reopen again that day. Sunday is the only non-working day in the markets. As for other, more conventional stores, remember the long lunch hours when you are planning your shopping trips. During the summer season (May 30-September 15), on Saturdays, the stores do not open again after lunch; they remain closed until Monday morning. Also, remember that shops stay open a little later in summer than in winter.

Emergencies

For medical and dental referrals, contact the United States Consulate at Lungarno Vespucci 46 (tel. 298.276). Also, most hotels in Florence maintain a list of English-speaking doctors and dentists.

The Florentine police headquarters is at via Zara 2 (tel. 477.901). For emergency assistance dial 113.

Florence also has an unusual First Aid organization, the Misericordia. Founded in the thirteenth century when family feuds and plagues were leaving a high number of disabled and dying people in the streets, this group of volunteers banded together to carry the wounded to hospitals and the dead to cemeteries. The Misericordia is democratic in membership. In the nineteenth century everyone in the Royal Family was a member; hundreds of craftsmen and laborers are also part of the historical register. To preserve the egalitarian spirit of the company all members wear long black robes (during the Middle Ages the garments were red) and black peaked hoods that cover the face with two holes for the eyes. With this disguise patients never know if they are being carried to the hospital by a count or a cobbler. Many towns around Florence have chapters of the Florentine Misericordia, but the members wear white robes and hoods. The headquarters for the Misericordia is in Piazza del Duomo 20 across the street and to the right of the Cathedral. Even if you're not in need of any medical attention, you're welcome to visit the headquarters and the church. It's customary to leave a small donation of a few hundred lire if a member of the Misericordia shows you around on a brief tour. The telephone number for emergency first aid is 212.222.

Worth a Detour

For a look inside a fourteenth-century palace walk over to the Museo della Casa Fiorentina Antica, also known as the Palazzo Davanzati. This Renaissance mansion is located at via Porta Rossa 13, a few blocks away from Piazza della Repubblica. The outside of the palace is embellished with the original rings for hitching horses, hooks for draping tapestries, rings for supporting flags and torches, and iron bars running across the second, third, and fourth floors where banners and rugs were displayed on feast days. Inside is the courtyard and family well, and behind this is a pilaster with the Davanzati coat of arms carved by the fifteenth-century sculptor Donatello. Climb up the stone steps to the first floor and the crimson-painted "Room of the Parrots." Here, splashed against the walls of this large dining hall, are bright fresco patternings borrowed from the ancient designs of medieval tapestries. Wander upstairs through the bedrooms and, if the fourth-floor loggia is open, walk out and take a look at the center of Florence as a Florentine merchant might have seen it. (The last family member to walk out on this loggia was Carlo Davanzati, in 1830. He threw himself over the railing and died a few days later.)

Back on terra firma you might want to take a short hike to Florence's nineteenth-century Moorish-style synagogue. From Piazza della Repubblica take the eastern axis from the ancient Roman plan of the city: via de' Speziali, il Corso, Borgo degli Albizi, and down via Pietrapiana; at the end of this street, turn left from Piazza Sant'Ambrogio onto via dei Pilastri. On your right look for via Farini and at no. 4 is the synagogue, surrounded by a Mediterranean garden of oleanders, magnolias, and luxuriant palm trees. Inside, the synagogue is a cool refuge of marble floors and great vaulted ceilings. The walls are painted to look like tiles; every inch is covered with Near Eastern geometric designs in lustrous colors of Pompeian red, turquoise, and bronze.

A small kosher restaurant is next door at no. 2/A (first floor). It's open from 12:00 noon to 2:00 P.M. and in the evenings from 7:00 to 9:00 P.M. (tel. 286.442).

There are two Florentine museums especially popular with children. The Museum of the History of Science is located in the fourteenth-century Castellani Palace next to the Uffizi Gallery in Piazza dei Giudici 1. Curiosity for the natural world and the heavens above was a hallmark of the Renaissance in Florence. The ten rooms of this museum are packed with early scientific equipment from the Medici collections and private gifts. Roam around the rooms of the first floor and you'll find in addition to some of Galileo's astronomical instruments many sundials, globes, calculators, clocks, binoculars, microscopes, and telescopes from the seventeenth up to the twentieth centuries. Many of the relics were damaged during the 1966 flood and some of the newly repaired equipment is displayed on the ground floor. The museum is open from 10:00 A.M. until 1:00 P.M. and from 2:00 to 4:00 P.M. It's closed the last Sunday of every month (tel. 293.493). A glittering collection of tapestries, furniture, and assorted artworks is displayed at the Stibbert Museum. What children find appealing is the medieval armor collected by the museum's nineteenth-century benefactor Frederick Stibbert. The Stibbert Museum is part of the Villa Stibbert, and to make things even easier the address is via Stibbert 26. The hours are 9:00 A.M. to 2:00 P.M.; it's closed on Thursdays (tel. 486.049).

✴If your walking shoes and stamina are up to it, buy a bottle of wine and hike up to Piazzale Michelangiolo in early evening. Sit on the steps of the thirteenth-century Romanesque Church of San Miniato al Monte and enjoy your picnic while the sun sets over the red-domed cathedral below.

Chronology

11th–8th century B.C.

Iron Age village of the Villanovian civilization; flooded over and buried by the Arno River.

59 B.C.

Founding of "Florentia," a military camp settled by veterans of Julius Caesar's battles; built on the model of the mother city, Rome.

1st–4th century A.D.

Christian religion began filtering into Florentia by means of Syrian and Greek traders; first Christian religious centers and cemetery were on the left bank of the Arno outside the city gates.

5th–7th century

Roman Empire weakening; Florence invaded by: (a) Ostrogoths: 405 A.D., (b) Byzantines: 539 A.D., (c) Goths: 541 A.D., and (d) Longobards: 570 A.D.; Longobards take over Florence and cut off the trade routes.

8th–10th century

Charlemagne, King of the Franks, defeats Longobards in 774; Florence annexed to Holy Roman Empire; beginning of growth as important medieval market town; scattered settlements and villages outside city walls (*borgi*).

11th–12th century

Florence grows into a "commune," a medieval urban corporation of merchants and traders joined together into guilds.

First half 13th century

Expansive economic and political growth of the guilds; Florentine families split into two political factions: the Guelphs, members of the merchant class who support the Pope, and the Ghibellines, the feudal nobility who back the German (Holy Roman) emperors.

Second half 13th century

Guilds in alliance with the papal Guelphs take control of Florence in 1280; this new power elite becomes the upper class or new bourgeoisie and displaces the feudal aristocracy.

14th century

1345: Cloth dyers go on strike.
1348: Plague of the Black Death, population is cut in half and slavery is legalized to increase the work force.
1378: Ciompi Riots; wool-workers revolt and take control of the government for two months, and then are defeated by middle-class merchants supported by wealthier merchants.

15th century

1433: Medici family gains power in Florence.
Girolamo Savonarola, a Dominican friar, assists in exiling the Medicis but in a countercoup is executed in 1498.

16th century

France and Spain are rivals for Italian peninsula; French move in and take over Florence until 1525 when Spanish overpower them; Medicis, as puppets to the Spanish throne, continue to rule nominally over Florence.

17th century

Spanish government continues to rule Italy.

18th century

1765: Uffizi Galleries open to the public.

19th century

Napoleon Bonaparte's exploits include the takeover of Italy.
1865–71: Florence is the capital city of Italy.

20th century

August 3/4, 1944: German High Command blows up all bridges in Florence with the exception of the Ponte Vecchio.
Postwar years bring new construction and burgeoning tourist trade to Florence.
November 1966: Arno River floods the city, damaging and destroying art collections and old buildings; Florentines dig out from under and start over again.

Walk

1

Dante's Florence

Starting Point: Corner of via de' Cerretani and Piazza San Giovanni (facing the Baptistery and Duomo)

An exploration of the oldest corners of Florence—Roman and medieval Florence—could begin nowhere else but where we are standing right now: on the corner of via de' Cerretani and the Piazza San Giovanni. If we were Roman legionnaires in the first century A.D., we might have come hiking down from Bologna or the Apennine Mountains and marched along the Cassian Way until we came to this exact spot. We would be at the northernmost gate of the walled town of Roman Florentia, a military camp given over to veterans of Julius Caesar's battles and a miniature copy, in almost every detail, of the mother city, Rome.

Once inside the city we could have walked a well-paved road that lies precisely under the twentieth-century sidewalk and that ran to the right of the Baptistery, straight toward via de' Pecori. We might have wanted to stop off at the Public Baths, which are several feet underground, sandwiched between the modern sidewalk and the Baptistery.

After freshening up at the baths, we could have strolled farther down the same road into the Forum, or town meeting place, which was directly under what is now the Piazza della Repubblica. If we were real pleasure seekers, we then might have headed outside the walls again and over to the theater (behind and under the Palazzo Vecchio) or to the amphitheater (just west of the Piazza Santa Croce), the outline of whose structure is still visible in the curving streets, to watch some anti-Christian sports complete with lions. Perhaps feeling penitent after our amusements, we would have dropped off at the temple of the Egyptian goddess Isis (a half a block from the amphitheater and next door to the theater).

Try to put yourself into the Middle Ages—if you haven't yet become totally unnerved by the whirl and screech of the sports cars, tourist buses, and motorcy-

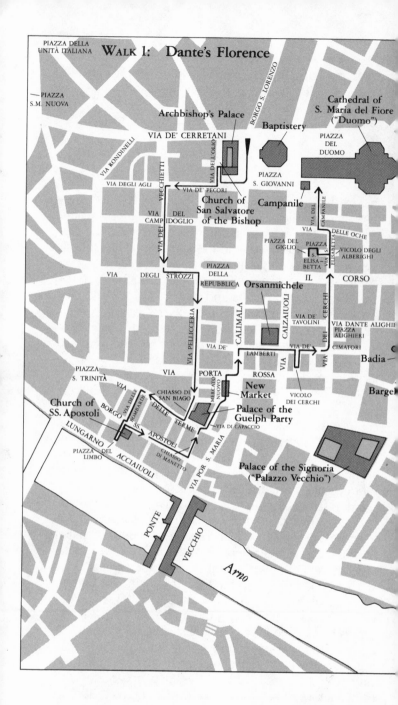

WALK 1: Dante's Florence

cles rounding the curve near the Baptistery and the
piazza. By the eleventh century a water-filled moat ex-
isted where via de' Cerretani is now and the town was
surrounded by an even larger wall. As medieval wayfarers or weekly marketers, we would be knocking on

another portal but in the same spot. This entrance to Florence would now be called the Bishop's Gate, because we would be coming into the religious center of Florence, a prosperous "commune," or medieval town, of the Holy Roman Empire.

Some time in the third century A.D. the Florentines stopped throwing Christians into their lion-filled amphitheater; by the next century they were putting up tiny churches around the outside of the town wall. When the Huns and Goths descended on Florence in the fifth century, the circumference of the town walls was shrunk to create a smaller area to defend. The little church of Santa Reparata was built in the fourth or fifth century beneath what is now the Duomo, and the Baptistery was probably begun in the seventh century. Both religious structures were outside the town walls, however, until Charlemagne liberated the Florentines from the Lombardian invaders and a new, much more expansive wall was built. The new wall wrapped around the Piazza San Giovanni and incorporated the two religious buildings into the town.

Scores of baptisteries were built all over northern Italy between the fifth and fourteenth centuries. The very first "baptisteries" were the riverbanks: Florence's earliest converts were more than likely baptized along the shore of the Arno near where the Ponte Vecchio is today; the first envoys of Christianity were the Greek and Syrian traders who camped out along the river's edge in the third and fourth centuries. Then, when the Romans decided to change their tune and join the church, the old Public Baths became the next location for holy baptisms. When the overflow of new Christians was too great even for the baths, the baptisteries were built, usually next to older churches.

By the eleventh century the Baptistery and the Piazza San Giovanni had become victims of urban sprawl. Street level was much lower than today. The Baptistery was raised, and had stairs leading up to the doors. To the north of the Baptistery was the city wall and Bishop's Gate; to the west and on the right of the sidewalk we're standing on was the original tenth-century Archbishop's Palace (the present sixteenth-century building serves the same function today). In the eleventh century an atrium and flower garden spread out in front of the palace, covering the sidewalk and old Roman

Baths. To the east of the Baptistery where the Duomo stands today was the church of Santa Reparata. South of the Baptistery was the cemetery—mounds of the most splendid Roman sarcophagi of carved and richly hued marbles. The coffins were secondhand, originally owned by the Romans who had placed them and their loved ones out on display along the major highways outside the cities. The Florentines dragged them from the roads and hauled them into the town for decoration and recycling. In 1296, when Arnolfo di Cambio was busy laying plans for the Duomo, he decided that the sarcophagi had to go, and most of them were hauled away. The piazza was repaved to cover the steps leading to the Baptistery, and the elegant marble paneling was added to the building.

In the thirteenth century this part of town was bustling and showy. Giovanni Villani, a famous chronicler of that era, reported some illuminating statistics from the tax records kept at the town gates: 55,000 barrels of wine passed through the doors in a good year, and 10,000 more barrels flowed through in an even better year. In addition, he reported that Florentines were eating "about 4,000 oxen and calves, 60,000 mutton and sheep, 20,000 she-goats and he-goats, 30,000 pigs and 4,000 loads of melons."

Walk along the piazza (the Baptistery on your left), past the Archbishop's Palace and down to the corner of via de' Pecori, named for an old but not particularly distinguished family who lived on this spot.

At this corner was once a great stone vault that stretched the entire width of the via de' Pecori. It was called the "Volta [Archway] of the Pecori" and it was a kind of architectural announcement that one was about to enter the territory of the Pecori family. We'll see two such archways still standing on Walk 2. The houses and towers of the family were attached to the archway and extended down the left side of the street.

Via de' Pecori and the next two streets on our walk appear today to be bastions of conservative commerce. Banks, offices, shops, and language schools line the streets. Don't be discouraged. The history of the streets is far more colorful than its twentieth-century semblance of propriety might lead you to believe.

Walk 25 yards down via de' Pecori and turn right onto via dell'Olio. You're now standing behind the

Church of San Salvatore of the Bishop (via dell'Olio)

block-long Archbishop's Palace and what was once the old market of the oil merchants.

About 25 feet from the corner of the street, and leaning out from the back of the Archbishop's Palace, is the little noticed but remarkable façade of a small eleventh-century parish church called San Salvatore of the Bishop. Cross the street to get a better look at the façade. The church was preserved and incorporated into the much newer Archbishop's Palace, but somehow over the centuries San Salvatore has begun to look more like the dusty backdrop for a Hollywood movie set. Art historians have almost forgotten the tiny church. One exception was Corrado Ricci, once curator of the Laurentian Library, who wrote in the early part of our century that San Salvatore was one of Florence's "bridge[s] between ancient Rome and the Renaissance." (The other "bridges" are the Baptistery and the Church of San Miniato.) The style of the thirteenth-century façade is known as Florentine Romanesque. The three arches forming an arcade at street level and the richly ornamented panels inside the arches with black-and-white checkered patterning make it Romanesque. It's Florentine because nowhere else in

Via de' Pecori

Western Europe was there such a simple but expressive use of these elements.

The church's special function in the Middle Ages was to serve as the center for the graduation exercises of the theological university. A candidate for the degree would arrive at the church dressed in his finest silks and velvets, accompanied by his family, friends, troubadours, jester, flutists, drummers, and horn blowers, and a motley array of more or less unacquainted well-wishers who had joined the parade along the way. After the successful completion of the examination inside the church, the new theologian and his entourage would proceed on, with the blaring music and merrymaking, to an entertainment—a joust, a play, or just a simple bacchanalian repast—provided at the expense of the graduate.

Walk back to via de' Pecori, turn right, and continue down the street. Look for the massive stone palace on the right side down near the corner. The first door will be no. 6. The second door, no. 8, is the one you should enter (if you've arrived during banking hours) for some unexpected splendor. This is the dazzling Palazzo Orlandini, now turned into the banking establishment of Monte dei Paschi di Siena. The pale frescoes, marble sculptures, and open courtyard are impressive, and a bit surprising in a bank.

Stroll over to the courtyard and look through the glass doors. Directly in front of you is the only fifteenth-century wall fountain in Florence that is still in its original location. Fountains of any kind, even for everyday use, were extremely rare in the fifteenth century. Wells and springs were Florence's only source of water five hundred years ago, and necessity, even for the very rich, came before embellishment.

The palace fountain, carved of *pietra serena*, represents a composite of styles developed throughout the fifteenth century. The naturalistic lion's head is probably from a later date. The *rocaille* work that fills the niche of the fountain is from the sixteenth century. Ironically, now that Florence enjoys an ample supply of water, this landmark fountain never seems to be in working order. A note of caution: Try to refrain from taking photographs inside any of Florence's banks unless you are interested in personally encountering a polite but anxious squad of security guards. (The photograph for this book was permitted only when the very serious, highly intellectual nature of the assignment was explained to the bank president.)

The actual room for the banking is to the right of this gracious "lobby." Walk inside and settle into some of the softest leather sofas that you'll ever come across. Notice the leather railing cushion around the tellers' counter, designed especially for pleasurable leaning during your business transaction. Above you, dangling from the ceiling, are hundreds of clear-glass globe lights. The Florentines take this comfort and elegance for granted; they expect their everyday business establishments to be as well put together and polished as their own homes.

If you're in a comfortable position, don't get out of the sofa yet. Read a bit more about the ancestral occupants of this neighborhood before moving on.

Via de' Pecori and its adjoining streets encircle what was once Florence's Roman Forum. As the centuries

Fifteenth-century fountain in "Monte dei Paschi di Siena"

passed, the Forum turned into a rambling medieval marketplace. In those early days of commerce, merchants lived over or next door to their work, and this meant the market. In the thirteenth and fourteenth centuries, the oldest and most prosperous families cornered the real estate of the marketplace. The names of the modern streets today bear the family names of the potentates who once built fortified compounds on via de' Pecori and along the next streets we'll visit: the Tosinghi, the Brunelleschi, the Agli, and the Vecchietti. The earliest branch of the Medici also lived a block or two away from this neighborhood, overlooking the market.

The first homes along via de' Pecori were dark strongholds with a few small windows and little ornamentation. Towers were built alongside the houses as fortification against attack from other families. A series of arches at street level joined one family house to another. They were called *archi da bottega*, "arches of the shops," and the owners of the houses either conducted their own business under them or they rented out the space to other merchants. We'll see some of these *case torre*, or "residence-towers," later on in the walk.

Farther up via de' Pecori were the next-door neighbors of the Pecori, the Tosinghi. A medieval record describes their thirteenth-century residence as "two hundred seventy feet high, made of thin marble columns, and a tower that was 300 feet high."

The population of Florence was constantly expanding and diversifying in the thirteenth and fourteenth centuries. Through the town gates came tribes of aspiring urbanites: retired farmers, impoverished nobility, deserting mercenaries, traveling pilgrims, mendicant priests, and Greek, Jewish, and Syrian salesmen. When the Black Death hit Florence in 1348, the community was swiftly cut in half. Florence badly needed to increase her work force after the plague's devastation, and in 1363 it was decreed that slavery would become legalized in the town. The gates opened once more and Tartars, Greeks, Russians, Circassians, Moors, and Ethiopians, already purchased in Venice or Genoa, were led into the workshops, homes, and even churches, to help shoulder the workload of a prosperous market town.

By the fifteenth century, via de' Pecori and the surrounding streets of the market were the scene of business transactions of every kind, many unsavory, carried out in alleyways and warehouses. The old families no longer found it fashionable or desirable to live near the market. After two or three hundred years of living where they worked, the merchants began to build new houses on the outskirts of Florence. They moved to the suburbs and left the city problems to the city dwellers. Their abandoned houses and towers were forced to serve new urban functions. A stone's throw away from the Archbishop's Palace, via de' Pecori became the entrance to the fifteenth-century red-light district.

A nineteenth-century historian, E. Grifi, sums it up:

> the locality was ill-famed; there were inns of the lowest order, two especially being notorious as the meeting places of dissipated characters of all varieties, the "Osteria del Frascato" ["The Inn of the Bower"] and the "Osteria della Malacucina" ["The Inn of the Bad Kitchen"]. Perhaps for that reason, and hoping to expel such shame from the centre of the town, Cosimo I chose this place when in 1571 he looked for an enclosed plot of ground where all the Jews residing in Florence could be assembled being thus set apart from the rest of the population.

The Jewish population was not on good terms with the rest of the town. In 1471, seventy Jewish merchants began two loan banks and within twenty years they had accumulated over eleven million gold florins. The understated Mr. Grifi remarks: "They began to be disliked by the people." Under Cosimo, a Medici duke, the Jewish men were required to wear a yellow badge on their hats and the women the same ornament on the sleeves of their coats and dresses. Their business privileges were curtailed and they were forbidden to deal in the wholesale market or in art objects.

This Ghetto remained the Jewish quarter for the next three hundred years; over the centuries the area expanded. By the mid-nineteenth century, when the Ghetto was torn down for the fine stores and offices that we see now, it had stretched as far as via dei Vecchietti (our next excursion).

Via degli Agli is the street directly across from the corner the bank is on. The Agli family moved onto the block sometime in the twelfth century, and they bought up half of the adjoining street, via dei Vecchietti. The Agli were an old, established family in Florence and it was natural that they would take a disliking to any *gente nuova*, or "new men," in town. Ceffo degli Agli called the fourteenth-century interlopers "*arteficiali de la merda!*" (A *very* refined translation would be "manufacturers of dirt.")

The Agli ran into a problem that many of the older families had to face: after centuries of breeding more and more Agli, a Florentine law decreed that every member of a family was responsible for the actions of all the other members of the family. This meant that if some third cousin clobbered someone, everyone related to that third cousin was guilty. If the clobberer ran off for parts unknown (which was frequently the case), the family had to pay a stiff fine or recruit another relative to serve the jail term. Things got out of hand by the mid-fourteenth century; practically everyone in Florence was liable for some crime perpetrated by a brother-in-law or great-nephew. So, a new law was thought up. People could change their names and no longer worry about the peccadilloes of their relatives. It seemed like a perfectly good solution to a sticky situation. Some of the Agli, along with dozens of other *grandi* ("great ones"), took on new names and new coats of arms.

The Agli, like most members of the upper class around the world, had servant problems. This is what one distraught husband, Aglio degli Agli, wrote to another relative (or perhaps a friend) in the fourteenth century:

> I had a very good slave, but, for her misfortune, she became pregnant and had a boy child—and since the father could not be found I took it and sent it out to nurse. But my Monna Lucia was seized with jealousy, and said it was mine; and though I told her it was only mine as a calf belongs to the man who owns the cow, she still will not believe me, whether I swear or coax. And she has won the quarrel, and the slave has been turned out, and we have now an old woman who is more like a monkey than a female; and this is the life I lead. So pray tell Monna Margherita to write a letter to Monna Lucia, so that she may not listen to gossip, and take back the slave, or at least get another who is not an old sow.

If you are outside the bank and back on via de' Pecori, cross the street, turn left, and begin walking down via dei Vecchietti, another street named for an old family who resided on the block beginning in the twelfth century. We'll come to their ancestral territory at the end of the street.

Via dei Vecchietti follows the same route as a paved Roman street under it. The Romans built Florentia according to a grid, and many of the present-day streets along this walk were originally planned by the Romans.

On the left side of via dei Vecchietti, about 15 yards from the corner, at no. 28 (where a branch of the Agli family once lived), is a venerable emporium, The Old English Store. It's a snug, wood-and-glass-cabinet reminder of the nineteenth-century Grand Tourers from the novels of Henry James and E. M. Forster who roamed the galleries and gardens of Florence and sketched in front of the Botticellis. Wilber & Sons Ltd. jelly jars line the shelves next to a healthy stock of international whisky and liqueurs. In the back are Scottish plaid skirts, Shetland sweaters, and French baby clothes. Florentines also favor this store. Tweedy, British Royal Family-type clothes are popular among the older members of the well-to-do. (The younger members are sticking to jeans, harem pants, and culottes at this writing.) The Old English Store has most recently been immortalized in short stories by the contemporary Italian writer Arturo Vivante. One of his characters, a spirited and independent-minded Italian matriarch, sports multiweave African shawls and Scottish skirts and sweaters from The Old English Store.

A few doors down at nos. 20–26 is another bank, the Instituto Bancario San Paolo di Torno, once an old palace. Take a look inside. The interior is rustic, subdued, and almost chaste in style. This bank will make you feel as if you are cashing your travelers' checks in a medieval cloister. Slices of stone wall from the original palace jut out from the twentieth-century cream-colored walls. Soft lighting and austere black leather hassocks also add to the monastic atmosphere.

Continue walking one more block along the left side of via dei Vecchietti. At the intersection with via degli Strozzi, you'll see a small bronze devil about 10 feet above the sidewalk on the corner of the palace

"The Devil's Corner" (via dei Vecchietti and via degli Strozzi)

outside wall. Since the Middle Ages, this spot in Florence has always been known as the Devil's Corner.

In Roman times, travelers entering Florentia by way of the Western Gate (where via dei Tornabuoni meets via degli Strozzi, and to your left if you are facing the devil) would have passed by this corner to come into the Forum. This intersection was also a Roman social center. In 1892 archaeological excavations uncovered the largest known Roman Baths here. The bathing establishment stretched 150 feet along via dei Vecchietti and 225 feet along via degli Strozzi. Flanked by the Roman Forum (facing left on via degli Strozzi where the Piazza della Repubblica is today) and the Capitol (on the present-day via del Campidoglio), the Baths were in a prime downtown location. This Roman institution was something like our urbane social clubs where political and financial contacts are made.

The palace on the left corner where the devil resides was the sixteenth-century home of some of the Vecchietti family. The Vecchietti (literally, "the Old Ones") moved into Florence sometime in the eleventh century and thereafter rose to civic prominence. One gentleman of the family was already a consul of Florence by 1128 and he may have set up house on this

street at this time. By the fifteenth century, the Vecchietti owned most of the land on both sides of the
street from the halfway point where the Aglis lived on
down to via degli Strozzi. The Vecchietti were also
well fortified with several palaces and towers. A thirteenth-century family patriarch was Marsilio, otherwise
known as the Knight of the Golden Spur. Some less
dashing members of the Vecchietti family were lucky
enough to have been placed in Paradise by Florence's
foremost poet, Dante, in his thirteenth-century opus,
The Divine Comedy:

> . . . and him of Vecchio, contented
> with their simple suits of buff; and
> with their spindle and the flax, the
> dames.
> *Paradiso* (Canto 15, line 115.)

Five silver ermines against a blue background was
the Vecchietti coat of arms. Less enlightened Florentines took the creatures on the arms to be rats. From
this misinformation there arose a peculiar saying in
Florence: When one becomes an old one (a Vecchietti) one is taking the arms of the rats.

Where did the roguish devil statue come from? He's
actually a copy of a sixteenth-century devil created by
a former resident of the palace, the Flemish sculptor
Giambologna, in honor of his patron and host, Bernardo Vecchietti. The original is on display in the Bargello Museum. Giambologna arrived in Florence in the
mid-sixteenth century with little to offer the city but
his talent. Bernardo took him in under this roof, and
in a short time the sculptor became something almost
unheard of in the art world: a living success.
Francesco, the Duke of Florence (and son of Cosimo I
who had moved the Jewish population to the via de'
Pecori ghetto), invited him regularly to court functions. Giambologna soon became the leading sculptor
for the city. His *Rape of the Sabines* in the Loggia dei
Lanzi of the Piazza della Signoria is probably his best-
known work in Florence though it has received mixed
reviews. One French critic called it "little more than an
alehouse scene . . . a husband knocked down, and a
soldier running away with his wife."

The original devil was created as a flag support for

the neighborhood banners that were displayed during the popular "Festivals of the Powerful" in the sixteenth century. These carnivals were organized every few months or so mainly to keep the working class in good spirits. An appointed leader of each neighborhood, or quarter, would take on the name and costume of an emperor, king, duke, or even a pope, and he and his cronies would then march and sing along the streets to the market or a piazza to meet the other "dignitaries" from other neighborhoods, and they'd all have a grand outdoor party.

Giambologna's devil would have been in a strategic place for these festivities. Directly ahead of us, to the right of the devil and at the end of via degli Strozzi, is the site of the Old Market. The Devil's Corner would have been the place for this neighborhood's merrymakers to assemble.

Giambologna designed a devil for the Devil's Corner, but why was this exact spot in Florence assigned to the underworld character? The matter is still open to scholarly debate. The most common explanation: one day in the mid-thirteenth century, St. Peter the Martyr was preaching on this corner. His sermon was on heresy and it was full of the usual fire and brimstone. Suddenly from around the corner appeared a large black horse, rearing and snorting flames of fire. Just as suddenly the horse dashed off again. Bystanders were sure that the animal was the devil himself.

My favorite story is another medieval tale often retold by an aged gypsy woman who frequented the Old Market in the last century before its demolition: there was a certain pious and very chaste lady-fairy who preached around in the streets of Florence, imploring the citizens to lead good and moral lives. It so happened that a devil, or imp, was also making his way around Florence, and when he heard of the unseemly competition of the lady-fairy, he decided to put a stop to it. He began chanting a certain verse around the Old Market that was meant to create an adverse impression of the good lady-fairy. The opening lines of the devil's song commenced by calling into question the good fairy's virtue:

'Tis that, while seeming pious, she,
Holding in hand a rosary,

> Her talk is all hypocrisy,
> To make believe to simple ears,
> That still the maiden wreath she wears.

To make matters worse, he even suggested that she was a seductress of other women's husbands:

> That dame who singing there you see
> Is a witch of this our Tuscany,
> Who up and down the city flies,
> Deceiving people with her lies,
> Saying to one: The truth to tell
> I know you love your husband well;
> But you will find, on close inspection,
> Another has his fond affection.

Now the fairy, who had good contacts in the ministry (some have suggested that it was the same St. Peter the Martyr), was able, through divine intervention, to change the devil into a *mascherone*, or architectural sculpture. And here he is today, or at least a copy of the original devil. There of course is a problem with chronology: the tale is said to be a medieval one, and Giambologna's statue was not even *created* until the sixteenth century. Some scholars, amateur and otherwise, have suggested that the corner has *always* been inhabited by devils, statues and real ones. On this note of uncertainty, we'll leave the corner and walk across the street to the photograph and old print shop, Alinari Bros.

Established in 1854, this gallery is the oldest and most respected business of its kind in Florence. Alinari Bros. is virtually synonymous with museum status. The family partners were way ahead of their time in recognizing the value of photographs as documentary records and as modern works of art. In 1896 the Association of Tuscan Prints praised the Alinaris' pioneer work in photographic documentation: "The Alinari Brothers opened new fields in photography and it is because of their accomplishments that today scholars can study works of art scattered in galleries and in churches in remote parts of Italy." The business is no longer in the hands of the Alinari family, but well-printed nineteenth-century photographs of Florence are still one of the chief attractions of this store. A visitor can spend hours leafing through the portfolios of photographs of the Old Market and river scenes of the Arno from a hundred years ago. (The photographs are 8 by 11 inches and sell for about $6 each.) One note of warning about the colored prints of birds and fruits and bucolic landscapes (and this was a warning given by the dapper salesman): they are old etchings yanked from antique books and expertly painted over by the art staff of Alinari Bros. The prints are mostly French, and begin selling at about $20. Very few Italian prints are for sale; they're rare and much more costly.

Continue walking down via degli Strozzi—in the direction of the arch over the street—until you reach Piazza della Repubblica, the former Roman Forum and Old Market of Florence from the tenth century through the mid-nineteenth century. Piazza della Repubblica is the oldest bit of land in Florence that has been continuously reserved for public use, whether for medieval trade and fortune-telling or the parking of cars and access to American Express today. On a warm, sunny day you may want to position yourself under the shade of the arcaded sidewalk on the corner of via degli Strozzi and via Pellicceria and read ahead about the history of the Old Market.

If there's one spot in all of Florence that could best represent the cultivation and courting of capital in the Middle Ages and the inevitable need to display the money in the form of the vast churches and artworks of the Renaissance, this is it. The Old Market was the nucleus of the business world and center for the growing number of powerful associations among merchants and craftsmen, the guilds. The history of Florence took an important turn with the formation of the guilds in the eleventh and twelfth centuries. They changed Florence from a sleepy inland river town into a medieval urban corporation, a "commune," and then to a famed, resplendent city of Western Europe.

The Old Market, throughout its nine hundred years, always held its medieval character and appearance but took on the burdens of overcrowding, overbuilding, and pollution. Four ancient churches graced the corners of the square and bestowed their blessings on the crowds of barterers and bargain hunters. Dozens of towers—some 80 feet high—belonging to the old families loomed along the sides of the piazza and over the stalls and pavilions, the benches and carts and stands

of the merchants. The arches of shops on the street below were rented out to the wealthiest merchants. As
space became costly, small alleyways between the
houses and towers were filled in with vaulted corridors where merchants kept their extra wares or
opened smaller "showrooms" and offices.

> The Old Market provides food for
> All the world,
> And carries off the prize from
> every other piazza.

So wrote Pucci, a fourteenth-century poet who lived in
Florence just after the days of Dante.

> Here on the side are the poulterers
> well-furnished in all seasons
> with hares, and boars, and kids,
> with pheasants, starlings, pigeons
> and all other birds.

In the midst of the feathered and furry market menag-
erie were the Medicis (from the Guild of the Physicians). Their house, with the shop on the ground
floor, was in the farthest left corner of the square directly under the shadow of the Duomo. The old medieval market was where they began their rise to fame
and fortune. It taxes our twentieth-century imagina-
tions to envision members of the medical profession
slinking around bolts of fabric and casings of sausages
while hawking their wares of good health, but this is
exactly what went on from the twelfth to the fourteenth centuries in Florence, then a very street-orient-
ed metropolis.

> And here were linen cloths,
> and flax merchants, pork vendors,
> and apothecaries . . .

The Physicians Guild and the Guild of Wool were two
of the most powerful economic and political groups in
medieval and Renaissance Florence; they were also
business allies. The physicians and pharmacists applied their chemical knowledge to perfecting the dyes
that made Florentine wools and silks so popular all
over the Mediterranean world. It was a natural enough
economic process for the Medicis to begin as men of
medicine, and then, as their wealth and business acu-

men increased, to branch out into banking, real estate, and politics.

For those who lacked the capital and know-how of the Medicis, there were ample numbers of moneylenders around the market to service the compulsive gamblers and their sport:

> Tables of ready-made money, and
> dice-players of every sort,
> that each may carry on his trade.

Moneylenders in the Old Market had a low overhead—a table covered with a green cloth, a wallet full of cash, and an account book. Their guild was called "The Company of the Table."

Five hundred years after Pucci's poem, the market had become cramped, dirty, and damp. The building of towers and storerooms and arches connecting houses and rooms over the arches had created a straggling warren of disorder and darkness right in the center of town. Cholera broke out in 1835. Fifty years later, the market, along with the forest of medieval towers that had grown up around it, was razed in compliance with a town ordinance.

Turn right into the arcaded and tile-floor passage of via Pellicceria. In the medieval and Renaissance days of Florence, this street was one of the busiest. It was filled to the brim with merchants' stalls and goods, and it was an example of how the overflow of people and products would spill into an adjacent thoroughfare. The name of the street recalls the furriers who once traded here. Via Pellicceria was also the goldsmiths' quarter until 1593, when Grand Duke Ferdinand I moved the artisans to the Ponte Vecchio. Ferdinand had had enough of the scruffy lot of butchers and blacksmiths and fruit and vegetable sellers who were cluttering up the oldest and potentially most picturesque bridge in Florence. Ferdinand evicted the marketers, moved in forty-one goldsmiths and eight jewelers, and started collecting twice the amount of royal rents. Shortly before the goldsmiths moved away from via Pellicceria, Benvenuto Cellini, the headstrong and homicidal future sculptor, was studying the gold-working craft on this street in a studio run by the father of Baccio Bandinelli, another illustrious Renaissance artist. Cellini was proud of his artistic talents and proud of his libertine life-style. His gambling, woman-izing, and murders kept sixteenth-century Florentine tongues wagging. In his autobiography Cellini recalls the remark of a visiting ambassador to his patron, Co-simo I: "That Benvenuto of yours is a terrible fellow!" "Yes," Cosimo replied, "he is far more terrible than you imagine." As for answering to his murderous mis-deeds, Cellini never had to worry. Pope Paul II very ef-ficiently pardoned his every indiscretion.

A walk down via Pellicceria today will yield one remnant of Old Florence's vices: gambling. Thirty yards from the corner, past the Banca Nazionale del Lavoro, and behind the archway, is the betting center: a lilac-roofed booth marked "Totocalcio." In the morn-ing hours of most days you'll see a respectable crowd of men and women milling around the betting booth and consulting the daily papers for upcoming horse and dog races. There's a far more relaxed—even jo-vial—atmosphere in the Florentine betting centers than in their American counterparts. Next door, the cavernous Post Office is a convenient place to mail any postcards that you may have just purchased among the jungle of newspaper stands that line this street. De-spite the air of tourism here, you'll still see, on a sunny day, a good turnout of mostly elderly gentlemen me-ticulously dressed in suits and vests. They'll be waving newspapers around and arguing over the latest politi-cal developments or the racing odds.

Via dei Lamberti is the small cross street just to the left of via Pellicceria and directly across from the en-trance to the Post Office. The Lamberti were an old German clan of nobility who first came to Florence in 962 with the Teutonic Emperor Otto II. This street was their family's territory. Legend has it that the Lamberti were not lacking in imaginative burial rites. One story describes their loved ones being interred in full armor and mounted on life-sized iron horses, thereby perpet-uating the warrior image. A slight embellishment to this tale is that the Lamberti constructed a large under-ground vault within the confines of their palace on this street and then furnished it with bronze horses and the skeletons of their ancestors. The Lamberti were the chiefs of the Ghibelline faction in Florence for a while. This meant that they were all for the Ger-man emperors and feudal nobility running things in town. Their opposition, however, was the Guelph party whose headquarters were, inconveniently, down the street. The Guelphs were made up of the increasingly wealthy class of merchants and guild officials. They supported the pope and whoever was sitting on the throne in France. There were a series of Charleses ruling in France from the thirteenth to the middle of the fifteenth centuries—Charles IV the Fair, Charles V the Wise, and Charles VI, either the Mad or the Beloved, depending on your point of view. The pope was happy, in turn, to support the Guelphs. He knew some up-and-coming young men when he saw them and the Florentine Guelphs looked like better bets for donating hefty tithes to the Church than the withering feudal nobility.

The Lambertis had a couple of centuries in Florence to build some impressive palaces, and then, sometime in the thirteenth century, they must have realized that their backs were against the walls with respect to the Guelphs. The family left town and were never heard from again around this neighborhood. Their lavish homes were taken over for various uses: headquarters for the oil merchants' guild, a pawnbroker's office, and, in the nineteenth century, before it was torn down, the Lamberti stronghold was converted into a fire and life insurance company.

Continue to the end of via Pellicceria and stop at the open square at the end of the street. This is Piazza di Parte Guelfa, the "Square of the Guelph Party." It's a milestone on this walk; original medieval and Renaissance homes now lie ahead of us most of the way. The ancient towers, narrow passageways, and placid palaces in the neighborhood around this piazza have survived modern urban demolition, ravaging floods, and the World War II bomber planes of the German High Command.

Pause in the square. This space is traffic-free. Sit down on the stone stairs that face the Palace of the Guelph Party, and take a good look at the building. It's the tall brick and stone structure that juts out to the piazza from the left corner of the square. A diagonal outdoor staircase crosses down in front of the building. The palace is a hodgepodge of architectural styles and idiosyncrasies accumulated throughout the twelfth, thirteenth, and fourteenth centuries. (Italian historians have nomenclature to describe each one of the centuries: the *Trecento* refers to the fourteenth century, the *Quattrocento* to the fifteenth century, and the *Cinquecento* to the sixteenth.)

The façade of the palace that is open to the piazza is the oldest section of the building. This part of the palace is like a short, squatter version of the medieval tower that has been referred to throughout the walk and will soon be seen around the corner from this spot. The large central mullioned window that is slit down the middle is ummistakably medieval. Several stone plaques with the Guelph family coats of arms are lined up above the window. Crowning the building is the crenellation (something like what we think of as topping a King Arthur castle). These squarish stones are architectural emblems of the Guelph party. The Ghibellines had their towers peaked with triangular-shaped stone ornaments.

The Guelphs fought the Ghibellines throughout the early decades of the thirteenth century. Political control of Florence was at stake. In 1267 the Guelphs, with the help of the French king, Charles of Anjou, defeated their rivals, and the reign of this merchant class began. The banking clients of the Guelphs, among others, were the French monarchy and the pope. Ghibelline property all over the city was confiscated. In 1277 the Guelph party bought this plot of land, built the tower, and stashed the Ghibelline stolen goods inside its walls.

The Guelph party was a dictatorial government in miniature. The half-dozen ruling families, some of whose houses and towers we'll pass in this walk, had the last word about everything important in Florence: who held offices, who could buy property, and who could charge what kind of interest rates. They organized and maintained the hospitals and markets, the churches and charities. Guelph ambassadors traveled to distant courts around Western Europe. Guelph leaders greeted and entertained all foreign dignitaries who came through Florence's gates. A chronicle dated February 8, 1386 describes how the Guelphs rode outside the city to welcome the ambassador from Hungary. After a jousting and flag-waving display in the Piazza della Signoria, ". . . they went to the Palace of the Parte Guelpha with much feasting and revelry." The

Guelphs managed to keep things under their thumbs for several centuries. By the mid-fifteenth century, however, the wealthiest families in the Guelph faction were engaged in a power struggle. In 1433 the Medicis won out and grabbed the reins of government. The more recent fifteenth- and sixteenth-century additions to the palace will be seen when we wind around to the other side of the building.

The very large palace to the right of the old Guelph headquarters is an ornate fifteenth-century Renaissance home complete with top-floor terrace. The two official addresses of this building are Piazza di Parte Guelfa 3 and, facing the next street we'll walk along, via delle Terme 2. Especially intriguing are the incised drawings, or *sgraffiti*, along the front of the house.

In the second half of the thirteenth century, Florentines first started building their palazzi or palaces. The ground floors of these grand residences were constructed of squarish-cut stones; the upper floors were less meticulously built. Oddly shaped stones, some retrieved from the riverbed of the Arno, were used to finish off the top floors. To conceal the irregularity in stonework the Florentines started to cover up the masonry in the fourteenth century with layers of stucco. Then, over the stucco, the artisans drew lines that resembled perfectly cut stones, a kind of trompe l'oeil in architectural decoration. Later on, in the fourteenth and especially during the fifteenth century, when this palace was built, the *sgraffiti* work became enormously popular. Incised drawings of flowers, cherubs, and scrolls became the rage, replacing the original fake-building-stone look. More palaces with this *sgraffiti* work will be seen on other walks.

Walk the few steps through the alleyway, chiasso di San Biago, and go past the 4-foot-high metal pole that sticks up out of the ground. Stop in front of the thirteenth-century medieval tower directly across from the *chiasso* ("alleyway") at via delle Terme 13.

Named for the original Roman Baths (*termae*) that are under the Palace of the Guelph Party, via delle Terme is one of Florence's very few remaining medieval enclaves. The passageway is narrow, shady even on sunny days, twisting, and stone-paved. Foot travelers, saddle horses, and donkey carts were the only traffic this street knew for many centuries. Today, only bicycles and the skinniest European cars will negotiate via delle Terme.

In the Middle Ages, streets such as this one were as narrow as possible because there were two opposing forces at work to secure every available inch of medieval Florence. Space was needed for markets, manufacturing, and traffic. At the same time, as the population grew and more and more families wanted to remain near the market and within the city walls, residential land became dear. The results of this conflict were narrow, constricting, irregularly shaped corridors such as via delle Terme.

In the eleventh century, well-to-do families began to build their homes and towers up and down this street. Via delle Terme and the next street on the walk, Borgo SS. Apostoli, were also the slaughtering and butchering center of Florence. The animals were killed right on the street, their blood dripping and spilling over the ribbonlike gutters now covered by the flat stones that line the side of the road. The carcasses were then skinned or plucked and carted up to the Old Market for sale. By 1319, though, the residents along these two streets decided that living in the heart of the slaughter district had lost its appeal. Citing health reasons, they were able to enact a law that prohibited the slaughter of the animals on their doorsteps, and the butchering industry moved for another century to the Ponte Vecchio.

The tower in front of us, at via delle Terme 13, is a model study in medieval Florentine architecture. Medieval towers in Florence started out as small single rooms usually built over Roman ruins. The dimensions were often as small as 10 by 15 feet. As a family's size increased, the room would be added on vertically rather than horizontally because there simply was no room to either side. A medieval town such as Florence was enclosed by a wall; a new wall would be expensive to build. So the space within the wall was probably comparable to midtown Manhattan—limited and sky-high in value. Some towers stretched as high as 240 feet, the comparable height of a ten- or twelve-floor apartment building.

The top floors of the tower were used as defense posts for the family during neighborhood feuds. The Buondelmonte clan, who once owned this tower, used to hurl crossbows down at their quarrelsome neighbors. By the fourteenth century, family feuds had quieted down somewhat, and the penthouse area was turned over to full-time living space. When their defensive purposes were outmoded, the towers were often altogether replaced in function by adjoining houses if the family could afford the extra space and building materials. (You'll see such a family compound on the next street.) The towers then became architectural symbols of the family's ancient ancestral status in Florence. A change in architectural styles, a shift toward the construction of palaces or palazzi in the late thirteenth century, caused the destruction of many of the hundreds of towers all over Florence. World War II bombings took care of most of the towers in this neighborhood with the few exceptions that we are passing.

The ground floor of the tower was always used as a shop or warehouse. A nineteenth-century historian once made the analogy that just as the foundation of the tower was always commercial, so was the foundation of Florence's civilization.

Notice the round holes resting on thick stone ledges that run along the second, third, and fourth floors of the tower wall. Wooden balconies, supported by beams, were hooked into these openings. On feast days, the family would drape rugs and fabrics from the balconies and watch processions from their temporary terraces. In the event of a family feud, all the finery plus the balconies would be hauled inside, the narrow windows barred, and arrows instead of banners would fly through the tower top.

Via delle Terme is a good street to walk down—head to your right—for at least two practical reasons. There's a casual, family-style restaurant called Nella at 19/r. A few yards away is a more subdued and expensive establishment, Ristorante al lume di Candela da Dante, at 23/r.

About 70 yards past this second restaurant look for your next turnoff on the left side of the street. It's another narrow alleyway, called via delle Bombarde. The street sign will be on the left side of the arch that we're about to pass through; it's 5 feet above eye level and often barely readable because little sunlight penetrates these alleyways. Make your way through via delle

Bombarde, cross the side street, Borgo SS. Apostoli, descend the five steps, and stop in front of the Roman-esque church to your left in Piazza del Limbo. This pi-azza is named for the unbaptized children who were once buried here. Charlemagne is said to have found-ed both the cemetery and the church, but it's doubtful that the church was begun by the king of the Franks. The Church of SS. Apostoli is an eleventh-century building that was refurbished in the fifteenth and six-teenth centuries and again in the years between 1930 and 1938. As members of one of the best-loved and best-cared-for parish churches in Florence, people in the congregation are always bustling around in the back behind the nave, clipping and arranging fresh flowers or polishing silver ornaments. The outside of the church is simple, almost severe. The front door dates from the fifteenth or sixteenth century. A plaque over the smaller wooden door to the left of the main entrance contains a Latin inscription that says that Charlemagne probably founded the church. A small roof extends over the door; a fresco once hung over the entrance and is now inside the church in the sec-ond alcove to the left. Brunelleschi is said to have used this church as a model when he designed the much grander Santo Spirito across the river.

The Church of SS. Apostoli was a medieval parish church. This means that unlike the large cathedrals that were built to make an awesome impression on the poorer folk of Florence, these tiny neighborhood churches were created for the daily needs of the peo-ple in this vicinity. Births, deaths, illnesses, and mar-riages were dealt with here. The parish church also served as a kind of town hall, judge's chambers, and sacred notary public. All business contracts and deeds were signed with the witness and blessings of the par-ish priests. From the very beginning of the earliest me-dieval era of Christianity, the church and commerce of every kind were insoluble business partners.

The first two columns directly inside the door of the church are capitals retrieved from a Roman hot spring. To the left of the altar is a tabernacle of glazed terra-cotta by Giovanni della Robbia.

Back outside in the piazza you'll see a plaque on the wall of the palace to the right of the church. This was the water level of the Arno River when the flood of

1966 filled up this tiny square. The church was swamped with oil-slicked water and mud, but the parishioners dug out and repaired every inch of the church.

To the extreme left of the church on the side wall of the next-door palace is a bas-relief of the Madonna and Child; another wall sculpture of Christ is above. These sixteenth-century urban art pieces were designed by Benedetto da Rovezzano, who was a favorite artist of the Borgherini family, the original owners of the palace. Other bas-reliefs and carved ornaments by this artist are on display in the Bargello Museum.

Turn the corner to your right and walk until you are standing in front of the palace that is Borgo SS. Apostoli 19.

This street is called a *borgo* ("borough") because the church and the houses on this block were outside the city walls during the Middle Ages. In this era everyone wanted to live inside the city walls, but because space was scarce, the leftover population clustered outside and within a few yards of the gates. Every day the gates would swing open and the *borgo* inhabitants rushed into the markets to buy or sell produce and goods. They always had to be on the outside of the gates by dusk when the town closed up or they would have to sleep in the streets and alleyways. A *borgo* was often a long extension of towers belonging to relatives or members of the same political faction. The line of towers could form a wall in itself facing the city wall and enclosing a new street, which is what we have here.

The palace we're standing in front of is best known as the Palazzo del Turco. It's an early sixteenth-century house designed by Baccio d'Agnolo, an architect who was also kept busy working out the plans for the flooring inside the Duomo, the tower for the Romanesque Church of San Miniato al Monte, and the belfry for Santo Spirito. The Palazzo del Turco is known for its legendary mistress. In 1529 when French troops entered Florence, a pack of soldiers made a beeline for this palace. It was famed for its delicately carved furniture by Baccio d'Agnolo and rooms full of paintings by the masters Grannacci, da Pontormo, and del Sarto. (All of the artwork is today safely ensconced in the Pitti Palace, the Bargello Museum, and the Uffizi Gal-

Borgo SS. Apostoli

lery.) The head of the family, Pier Borgherini, was out of town when the French arrived at the door demanding that they be let in to loot the treasures. The door remained bolted while the lady of the house, Margherita Borgherini, busily lined up her household help for battle. Pots and pans, chains and irons were hurled down at the French soldiers from the small-paned windows of the top floor. The soldiers surrendered under attack and walked away from the collection.

Across the street from the Palazzo del Turco is an unusual sight for downtown Florence: a large iron-grille gate with an open view of a private garden complete with sculptures of stone squirrels and birds perched on Ionic columns and pedestals. This garden also happens to be the scene that eighteenth-century American painter Benjamin West would wake up to see every morning from his studio window (at the upper right). West's life was the artistic and social success story of the eighteenth century. The son of a Pennsylvania innkeeper, West went on to become the president of the Royal Academy in London. During his rise, he invented the *camera obscura*, sketched, painted, and fought off Indians with Mad Anthony Wayne. There are numerous conflicting reports of just exactly what West was doing in Florence. One biographer says that West was suffering from a "nervous illness" and also that his leg was injured. After an eight-month confinement in the Italian port city of Leghorn, he managed to drag himself to Florence. Members of the British nobility reportedly visited his bedside while he recuperated. Another writer mentions that West, in his Borgo SS. Apostoli studio, was hard at work on a portrait of Lord Byron. Still one more historian with a more romantic bent informs us that West was desperately lovesick ("nervous illness"?!) over his American fiancée, Elizabeth Shewell, whose father had forbidden them to meet for five years. They later married in 1765, five years to the day.

At no. 12 is a pair of nineteenth-century Egyptian sphinx doorknobs. Napoleon's adventures in Egypt greatly excited the Florentines. A rage for mummies, snakes, pyramids, and sphinxes developed, and the motifs appeared all around the city.

At Borgo SS. Apostoli 9/r-9 is a fourteenth-century

Sculpture garden (Borgo SS. Apostoli)

palace that once belonged to the Acciaiuoli family. This clan owned most of the property along the street and all the way back to the Arno. They arrived in Florence around 1160, got involved with city politics, and then were thrown out of town in 1326 after a feud with another family. Returning in 1342, they tried for and managed a political comeback. One Angiolo Acciaiuoli, a Dominican friar, became the Bishop of Florence. The most noted member of the family, though, was Niccolò, who sought his fortune in Naples and later increased his fortune as the paramour of Catherine, the empress of Constantinople. The Acciaiuoli also kept up a few estates in Greece.

Across the street at the corner of chiasso delle Misure is another Acciaiuoli residence. The tower, no. 18/r, dates from the thirteenth century, and the connecting palace, no. 20/r, is a fourteenth-century addition. This kind of living arrangement is an example of what you read about a short while back. The tower was the original home and defense system for the Acciaiuoli, and the house was a modernized extension. The Pensione Norma is located inside this palace, and its address is no. 8. If the door to the pensione is open, walk through the lobby and look at the Acciaiuoli coat of arms etched into the glass windows on the door to the courtyard.

A branch of the Buondelmonte family lived at Borgo SS. Apostoli 6. This is the oldest palace belonging to the celebrated family—we'll hear more about them at the next stop. The proximity of the palace to the territory of the Acciaiuoli clan indicates a strong social tie. In fact, the two families intermarried so often they were almost the same clan.

Look for no. 3, and then pause in front of the building to the right of this address. You'll see, on the ground level, the remains of a thirteenth-century Buondelmonte tower. The floors above are a post–World War II addition—the top half of the tower was blasted off by the Germans in 1944.

Some seven hundred years before, in 1215, a marriage of convenience and political alliance was arranged between the young heir to the Buondelmonte family who lived at this tower residence and a daughter of the rival Ghibelline clan, the Amidei. Shortly before the nuptials were to be performed, the betrothed Buondelmonte dei Buondelmonti was passing by another home tower of an equally distinguished family, the Donati. The female head of the Donatis called sweetly down to Buondelmonte from an upstairs window and asked him to step inside the tower for a minute. He agreed. Waiting for him in the sitting room was an alluring young Donati maiden decked out in her finest maiden's attire. One thing led to another and Buondelmonte decided to replace his Amidei bride with the Donati lass on his appointed wedding day. The Amidei did not take this switch in marriage partners lightly.

It was a splendid spring morning when the groom sauntered out of this house for the wedding. The streets and towers were decorated with flowers and flags, swaths of silk, and displays of Oriental rugs. The entire town stopped to watch the wedding parade. The bride and bridegroom, dressed in white velvet and brocade with crowns of flowers on their heads, rode through the streets of Florence on milk-white horses. Musicians, singers, and finely attired friends and family followed behind them. As the wedding party began to squeeze its way over the narrow Ponte Vecchio toward the church across the road from via delle Terme, a band of Amidei sprang out from behind their tower, jumped on the bridegroom, and stabbed his white robes with their daggers until he bled to death before the crowds. Buondelmonte's body was arranged on a makeshift bier with his head in the lap of his bride, and the procession continued through the streets. The music-making changed to a mournful dirge; the merrymaking changed to shouts for a bloody revenge on the Amidei. Florence's ruling clans quickly split down the middle over the event. Thirty-nine of the most powerful merchant families sided with the Buondelmonti; thirty-three clans of the feudal nobility aligned themselves with the Amidei. The two groups had been grappling for power for decades, and the murder of the Buondelmonte bridegroom pro-voked bloodshed between the Florentine families for many more decades to come.

Glance up at the plaque on the second floor of the Buondelmonte tower. The quote is an excerpt from the *Divine Comedy*; it was written a generation after the still-notorious murder:

> o Buondelmonte, quanto mal fuggisti
> le nozze sue per li altrui conforti!
> Molti sarebber lieti, che son tristi,
> se Dio t'avesse conceduto ad Ema
> la prima volta ch'a città venisti.

> *Paradiso* (Canto 16, lines 140–144)

A rough translation is: "O Buondelmonte, what ill luck that you fled your own betrothed when another beck-oned; many more people would be happy who are now sad if God had let you drown in the Ema [a river outside of Florence over which the Buondelmonti must have passed on their first arrival in Florence] when you came to the city."

From the Buondelmonte tower walk about 15 feet, turn left, and then left again down chiasso di Manetto. At this corner is a moderately priced trattoria. If you don't stop for a meal, keep strolling down chiasso di Manetto until you reach via delle Terme. Turn right and walk only about 20 feet until you come to the left-hand turnoff of via di Capaccio. A side wall to the Pa-lazzo di Parte Guelfa will be on your left and a sidewalk café with a brown awning on your right. The name of via di Capaccio probably comes from the Latin *caput aquae* meaning the "head of the water." An aqueduct, providing the water for the Public Baths, ran through this street.

As previously promised, we see on the left side of via di Capaccio the fifteenth- and sixteenth-century additions to the Palazzo di Parte Guelfa. This side of the palace was added onto the fourteenth-century tower that we saw in Piazza di Parte Guelfa. Brunelleschi, the fifteenth-century architect of the great red dome on the Cathedral of Santa Maria del Fiore, began the design of this side of the palace; it was later finished by Francesco della Luna. Giorgio Vasari, whose sixteenth-century book *Lives of the Artists* is a mine for Florentine gossip about the Renaissance art world, designed the small hanging balcony, or loggia, at the far end of the building. Inside the loggia is a polychromatic stone coat of arms of the Medici family created by Giambologna.

At the end of via di Capaccio is the Mercato Nuovo, or "New Market," a large open loggia full of straw goods designed especially with the visitor to Florence in mind. The New Market was built under Cosimo I, the same Medici who in the sixteenth century confined the Florentine Jews to the Old Market area. The New Market was to be the silk and gold center, and the neighborhood around it was the financial district of Florence. Bankers and merchants of every kind congregated in the New Market. The two most important guilds in Florence, the Silk Guild and the Wool Guild, had their headquarters a block away from the New Market. The Old Market represented the beginnings of a medieval commercial system with exchange of goods and produce; the New Market is the Renaissance result of the growth of the guilds. Wool, silk, and banking (that is, money-lending at healthy interest rates) were the roots of the Renaissance splendor of Florence.

Fourteenth-century Florentines had some interesting business advice to pass on. For the would-be self-employed:

Labour always rather for thyself than for others.

For inheritance and trust fund victims:

Know how to keep and guard that which hath been left thee by thy father or other kindred. Money which a man

> hath not earned is more quickly spent than that which he
> hath earned with the sweat of his brow . . .

And some consumer advice:

> Give good heed to the small sums thou spendest out of
> the house, for it is they which empty the purse and con-
> sume wealth and they go on continually. And do not buy
> all the good victuals which thou seest, for the house
> is like a wolf, the more thou givest it the more doth it
> devour.

Walk to the center of the New Market and look for a
small round slab of marble on the floor. It may be covered over in part by the booth of a straw merchant.
The marble inlay is in the design of the wheel of a cart;
the background is white, and the spokes of the wheel
are pale gray. This was the spot around which all the
bankrupt businessmen, those who didn't heed the
proverbs, would have to sit. Occasionally a pantaloon-
less debtor would be hauled up by a rope attached to
the roof of the market, the rope loosened, and the vic-
tim thrown down on the cold, marble slab. Another
peculiarity about this market is that no one was allowed to carry arms of any kind within its boundaries.

Walk out of the New Market, turn right, and cross
the street at the corner of via Porta Rossa and Calimala.
Continue walking down the left side of Calimala for 25
yards until you reach via de' Lamberti. Stop at this
corner for a moment. This territory we're covering,
from the New Market to via de' Lamberti, was called
in Renaissance days Il Baccano, the "place of up-
roar." Younger merchants, some even just small boys,
would have stalls and wares spread out all over this
block; their shouts and entreaties to passersby led to
the nickname.

The Cavalcante family had their palaces on this
street. Guido Cavalcante was Dante's great friend, and
the poet, who lived only a few blocks away, strolled
along this street to meet Guido at the house of the Ca-
valcantes.

Calimala was where the old workshops of the foreign wool merchants were located. The name of the
street may come from the Greek word for "beautiful
fleece." Rough, uncolored fabric was brought across
from the Alps to Florentine workshops where exotic
dyes of deep purples and reds were applied. Then the

finished product was sent back across the Alps to England, France, and the Netherlands, and a hefty profit was made by the merchants of this city. Guido Biagi, a nineteenth-century chronicler of Florentine life, wrote that for Italian merchants "France was the America, the California of those times, and whoever returned thence with a full purse put on airs of great pride." The following is a verse that Biagi discovered and translated:

When Neri Picciolin came back from France
He was so full of florins and pride
That he looked upon men as poor little mice,
And each he did mock and deride.
He frequently cried, "Now may evil befall
All my neighbors, for seen face to face
With me, they appear but so mean and so small
That their friendship will bring me disgrace."
Soon this conduct was cause, I have heard,
That no neighbour, how e'er mean and low,
But scorned to speak him a word,
And I'll wager my heart for a crown
That before eight months had gone by,
He'd have thanked for a crust flung him down.

Walk across via de' Lamberti so that you are standing on Calimala facing the fashionable clothing store Zanobetti with its bright blue and gold awnings. Zanobetti is housed in the old Palace of the Wool Guild, built in 1308. Look over the third awning on your right. The wall sculpture of a lamb carrying a flowing banner was the official emblem of the Wool Guild.

Cross Calimala and walk 25 yards past the gleaming shop windows of the silver store Arte Fiorentina. Across the alley, and next on via de' Lamberti is Orsanmichele, a fourteenth-century church that stands on the site of what once was an eighth-century orchard and vegetable garden. This part of the street is now a vehicle-less walking mall. Stop and read a bit further while resting on the wooden benches in front of Orsanmichele.

In the center of the eighth-century fields on this spot was a small church dedicated to Archangel Michael. Produce from the gardens and imported corn were sold in a small market near the church. The name Orsanmichele comes from either *hortus*, a garden, or the

Emblem of the Wool Guild (via Calimala 3)

Latin word for granary, *horium*. A covered market, similar in structure to the New Market, was built here, but it burned down in 1304. Another covered market was begun in 1307. After the plague of 1348, the grateful survivors of the disaster poured money into the building of a church incorporated into the market. At the end of this century, though, the town fathers decided to move the mercenary activities somewhere else and the building became solely religious in purpose. Surplus grain for the town's populace was kept in the top floors through the sixteenth century.

From the via de' Lamberti side of the church, you'll see four tabernacles that were installed by the guilds of Florence. On the corner closest to via Calimala is the tabernacle of St. Mark from the Guild of Flaxdressers and Secondhand Dealers. Next is a fifteenth-century statue of Saint Jacob provided by the Guild of Tanners and Furriers. The doctors and apothecaries put up the Madonna in the third niche. Unlike the stone figures in the other niches, the statue of St. John the Evangelist at the far corner is made of bronze. Naturally, the most powerful guild, that of the silk merchants and goldsmiths, commissioned a more costly figure for display.

Renaissance Florentines were forbidden to make noise or gamble around Orsanmichele. Anyone who ignored this edict was either sent to prison or subjected to a public "baptism"—thrown off one of the bridges into the muddy waters of the Arno.

After this chilling thought you may want to cross the street and have coffee at A. Manaresi on the right side of via de' Lamberti. This is a famous Florentine café, established in 1898 but recently remodeled. The big attraction at Manaresi are the gold pipes that stretch from the ceiling to the countertops and look like a convention of tubas stretched out and suspended in midair. Ground coffee comes shooting out of these pipes, and they are the only remaining artifacts of the nineteenth-century décor.

Walk to the corner of Orsanmichele where via de' Lamberti meets via Calzaiuoli. In the fifteenth century, Florence was famous for its manufacture of serge stockings, or *calze di rascia*, and via Calzaiuoli was then named in honor of the trade's hosiers. The French emperor, Charles V, was conspicuously wearing a pair of these serge stockings when he made his triumphal entrance into the city in 1536.

Cross via Calzaiuoli (it's also vehicle-less), and walk to the corner where the street meets the narrow via de' Cimatori. Turn for a moment and face Orsanmichele.

Via Calzaiuoli was once divided up into little sections with separate street names according to the various market activities that were taking place along the route. In Renaissance times, the area from the point where you are standing down to Piazza della Signoria

Nineteenth-century brass coffee shoots at A. Manaresi

on your left was called via Cacciajoli or "Street of the Cheesemongers." The part of via Calzaiuoli on your right was known as via dei Pittori, or "Street of the Painters." Here artists would set up booths with paintings and await commissions from the merchants and foreign businessmen who strolled by on their lunch hours. Many painters during the first half of the fifteenth century were considered to be craftsmen, and they worked and did business in the company of furniture carvers, weavers, and potters.

The small fourteenth-century church on this corner is called San Carlo. The architects of the Duomo, Simone Talenti and Benci di Cione, also designed this church.

Begin walking down via de' Cimatori. We're now about to enter the real back alleyways of Florence. Ten feet from the corner, at no. 38/r, is Chianti Così ("Chianti Here"), a wine bar worth pausing at. Like most of the increasingly rare wine bars still in existence in Florence, Chianti Così is frequented mainly by Florentines. But don't turn away. The bartenders are friendly, and the wine selection is first class. Also, like all genuine wine bars, there are no tables and chairs. Italians take their "wine break" as they take their espresso—standing up. You may want to follow the example of the younger Florentines: take your glass of red or white wine and a *panino,* or "little sandwich," and sit on the steps of the apartment house across the street.

For a more substantial repast, there's a trattoria a few doors down at no. 30/r called Da i Cinque Amici. The prices are very reasonable for a simple but acceptable lunch or dinner.

Walk 25 yards down via de' Cimatori and turn to your right for a brief detour to vicolo dei Cerchi 1. This *vicolo* (or "little passageway") between via de' Cimatori and via Condotta is another example of how social change affected the face of the city. Every once in a while families such as the Buondelmonti or Acciaiuoli fell on hard times and were forced to sell some of their palaces and towers. The family block or compound was then broken up by the new family in residence. The Cerchi once owned a continuous wall-to-wall street of buildings on either side of this *vicolo* along via de' Cimatori. When they needed extra cash, they sold some of their homes and this little alleyway was carved out between the unrelated families to establish some breathing space. The *vicolo,* such as this one of the Cerchi, are representative of the ragged, sometimes cramped byways of Florence that are hidden behind the wider, well-traveled streets.

At vicolo dei Cerchi 1 is a thirteenth-century medieval palace of the Cerchi family that's fairly well preserved.

The Cerchis were travelers and traders in Western Europe and North Africa, and they were titans in Florence. They once owned all the land from Piazza San Firenze across to this corner, and up to the next cross street, via de' Tavolini.

Return to the via de' Cimatori, to the intersection with via dei Cerchi. Across from the tabernacle with the hanging lamp is another Cerchi palace. Imbedded in the corner facing the intersection is a pillar from the family loggia, or porch. The ground-level floors of most towers were generally rented out to artisans, but a tower at a corner intersection such as this one was far too strategic to waste on a store. This space was reserved for the loggia where male members of the family conducted business and female members entertained guests. This corner spot was also ideal for keeping an eye on city and neighborhood events. The bottom floor of the tower often stretched out into part of the street, and then pillars were added at the sides to support a roof extension. Later, more elaborate loggias were built as separate structures from the family house. Usually they were situated across the street and facing the palazzo.

Make a left turn at the intersection and continue down via dei Cerchi. In warm weather and during morning hours, outdoor vegetable stands line this narrow road, and marketers are always scurrying in and out of the cheese and wine and meat stores that stand elbow-to-elbow along this route. A twelfth-century tower sits at the corner of via dei Cerchi and the next cross street, via de' Tavolini. Around lunchtime in the small Piazza Alighieri to your right, you're sure to see a street vendor behind a *trippaiolo*, a booth stocked with mouth-watering tripe sandwiches. At the end of this street is a reconstructed version of Dante's house. If you didn't fill yourself up with tripe, there's the restaurant Da Pennello at no. 4/r. Another nearby restaurant is Antico Barile at via dei Cerchi 40/r.

The next street that crosses via dei Cerchi is Il Corso. In Roman days it was the Decumanus Maximus, a wide street that divided the city precisely into quadrants. In the fourteenth and fifteenth centuries, races were held along Il Corso. Crowds would line up along the street to watch stallions without jockeys fly down Il Corso eastward toward Borgo degli Albizi. The owner of the winning horse received the Palio, a richly woven cloth. Later, the yearly event was enthusiastically referred to as the Palio.

Via dei Cerchi crosses Il Corso, turns slightly leftward, and then becomes via Santa Elisabetta. Two adjoining twelfth-century towers are on your left between Il Corso and the small open square of Piazza Santa Elisabetta. A sixteenth-century parish church dedicated to Santa Elisabetta once stood in this square. Next door to the church, and down, were the headquarters of the official city trumpeters of Florence. You'll see an old street sign to the left of the square that reads "Piazza San Michele delle Trombe"; it's left over from this era.

Look above the piazza and you'll notice a very unusual thirteenth-century tower: it's round and known as the Pagliazza. Female prisoners were interred in this tower. The name refers to the straw (*paglia*) beds that they slept on.

A leather shop at no. 8/r complete with a French-speaking (but also English- and Italian-speaking) leather craftsman overlooks the piazza.

For a very peculiar detour, walk through the alleyway to the right of the round tower. Continue past the open iron-grilled doorway; turn left down a short corridor; and turn left again. This is the postage-stamp size square Piazza del Giglio. It's always as still as night inside this *real* back alleyway, except for an occasional group of gossiping marketers or businessmen cutting through on their way to lunch. Monuments to saints and a priest and a few stone plaques line the side walls of this square. The most startling piece of artwork is a Cubist-looking wall monument to John Fitzgerald Kennedy, *"il presidente della Nuova Frontiera."*

Retrace your steps and walk back to Piazza Santa Elisabetta.

To the right of via Santa Elisabetta and the piazza is the vicolo degli Alberghi, one of the very few medieval passageways extant in Florence. Notice the bridgelike room over the alleyway. This served as a link between the houses of families who were related by kin or marriage. On the corner of this *vicolo*, at no. 6/r, is Ottorino, a moderately priced restaurant.

Continue just a few feet down via Santa Elisabetta. Turn left on via delle Oche, "The Street of the Geese." At no. 20/r is one more medieval tower, the thirteenth-century home of the once-powerful Visdomini family. The clan had an unusual privilege in Florence: one of the duties of the Bishop of Florence was to oversee the collecting of taxes for the church coffers. If the position of bishop happened to be vacant, the fund-raising job fell to the Visdomini family. When a new bishop was elected, his first obligation was to honor the Visdomini for their invaluable services. A magisterial procession of costumed church officials was assembled at the Archbishop's Palace; the parade of clergymen marched over to this tower and then retired inside the walls for a hearty state banquet.

Via delle Oche is the street along which the earliest circuit of city walls was uncovered in archaeological excavations. Remember that the Baptistery and the small church of Santa Reparata (under the Duomo) were outside these walls until the eighth century. At this time new walls were built to include the religious structures within the fortified town.

You can see via Calzaiuoli at the end of via delle Oche. This corner was a hangout for the rich but idle youth of Renaissance Florence. The spot was nicknamed "La Neghitosa," the slothful.

Turn right onto via del Campanile. The other name for this alleyway is worth a moment's thought: via del Morte, or "Street of Death." Boccaccio, the popular fourteenth-century Italian storyteller usually associated with far lustier material, furnished this explanation for the name of the street: a young lady of noble birth named Ginevra was in love with a gentleman named Rondinelli, but as one might predict in these stories her father forbade her to marry him. She was instead betrothed to the son of a family friend, Francesco Agolanti. A plague struck Florence in the mid-fourteenth century and Ginevra fainted almost but not quite dead away. Her husband, Francesco, assuming that she had expired, had her buried in one of the Roman sarcophagi in the cemetery next to the cathedral. Sometime later, on the night of her burial, Ginevra recovered only to find herself in a bad predicament. But she did manage to push off the top of the sarcophagus and start to make her way home to her husband's house. Ginevra walked through via del Morte on the way to Francesco's. When she knocked at her husband's door, however, Francesco jumped out of his pajamas at the sight of what he thought was his wife's ghost, and he refused to let her in the house. Ginevra then moseyed over to her father's house near the Old Market but the same reception awaited her there. Last but not least, she proceeded toward the house of her former lover, Rondinelli (on the street with the same name located near the beginning of this walk). Naturally, he was joyful to see her. His family welcomed her into their home. A few days later, a judge in the courts decreed that as Ginevra had officially died and was buried, her first marriage was thereby annulled. She was free to marry Rondinelli and live happily ever after in Florence.

At the end of via del Campanile—also the end of our first walk—is the Piazza del Duomo.

Walk

2

Streets of the Renaissance Princes

○

Starting Point: Piazza del Duomo and via
Ricasoli

Our second walk begins at the north corner of Piazza
del Duomo where via Ricasoli begins.

In the Darkest Ages of Florence, fruit orchards
stretched out behind the city walls and over via Ricasoli. In medieval days this thoroughfare was called via
del Cocomero, the "Street of the Watermelon." It was
also the address of the thirteenth-century painter Cimabue and his apprentice Giotto, who took over his master's house and studio when he died in 1302. As
Florence changed from a provincial river town into a
medieval urban commercial center, this street and
those around it were plowed up and transformed into
artisans' workshops. The streets closest to the Duomo
resounded with the sounds of hammering and tapping
and hissing of forges and bellows. Via Ricasoli was
also the casket-making center of the town. A block
north of here, at the intersection with via de' Pucci,
were the workrooms of the tinkers and coppersmiths.
The next street over to our right, via de' Servi, was the
territory of the furniture and box artisans. A little north
of them were the studios of the bit- and bridle-makers.

The 125 yards or so of via Ricasoli that we'll be
walking along was a fashionable nineteenth-century
strip. It was very much a part of the theater and bistro
district.

On the left side of the street, at no. 3, is the Teatro
Niccolini, named for Giovan Battista Niccolini, a passionate political poet who wrote to further the "Risorgimento," the nineteenth-century movement to unify
all of Italy. Built in 1652, the theater has had a couple
of nicknames. First it was called Il Cocomero, "The
Watermelon," after the name of the street. Then the
resident dramatic society renamed the building the Accademia degli Infuocati ("The Academy on Fire").
Look above the door and over the second floor at the
equally unconventional coat of arms: a stone-carved
lighted bomb. Fifteen hundred people could while
away the night at The Academy on Fire. A stuffy nineteenth-century account says:

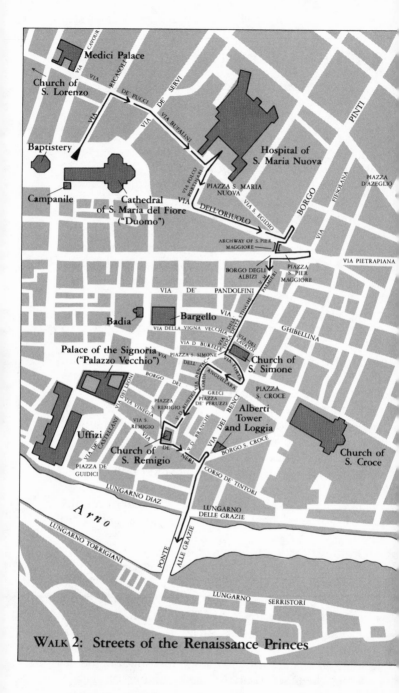

WALK 2: Streets of the Renaissance Princes

It is the leading theatre for Dramatic companies during the winter, frequented by the best society. Almost every year French plays are given by the best Artists from Paris, and sometimes during the winter good operas by ancient masters.

Since the days of the sixteenth-century pageantries of the Medicis, Florentines have always loved drama and show. The glossy, glamorous nightlife of the theater world was a passion for nineteenth-century Florentines, especially during the bleak and chilling winter season. In 1824 the Grand Duke of Florence, Ferdinand III, lay on his deathbed. His parting words to his son were: "Take care of my wife, of your sister, and of my people." As an afterthought he said: "In these circumstances the theaters are always closed for a long space of time, but many people who earn their bread in that way suffer from this. Shorten the court mourning." Before leaving the theater, check the listings on the front of the building. There may be a midday concert or evening play about to be performed.

At no. 9 was the home of the Baron Bettino Ricasoli, a nineteenth-century celebrity and the figure for whom the street was named. Ricasoli was born in Florence in 1808, descended from a twelfth-century family of nobility. A latter-day Renaissance man, he was a farmer, journalist, mayor (of Florence), and finally a minister of the government of Tuscany during the unification of Italy.

Walk to the corner at the left of via de' Ricasoli and via de' Pucci. Against the wall of the house on the corner is a tabernacle, or religious shrine, with two barely visible glass-enclosed paintings. The Madonna on the left is by fifteenth-century artist Filippino Lippi, the Madonna on the right by fourteenth-century painter Buffalmacco. The house against which the tabernacle is built was at one time the home of Giotto and his compatriot Buffalmacco. Legend has it that the latter painter was more famed for his sense of humor and practical jokes than artistic talent. This tabernacle—the Tabernacle of the Five Lights (Tabernacolo delle Cinque Lampade)—is actually one of the most famous in Florence. In the nineteenth century it was the clock at the Hotel Biltmore, the meeting place for socialite Florentines.

Tabernacles were originally set up in marketplaces and on streetcorners in the medieval days. Shoppers and artisans would stop in front of this tabernacle on their daily rounds. A brief prayer would be said and maybe a few flowers deposited on the ledge.

Under the paintings is a marble slot with the word

Elemosine ("Alms") carved on it. A few coins are often dropped into the slot as an offering to the poor. In medieval days, the act of almsgiving was not an altruistic gesture. The giver of the alms was supposed to be rewarded for his generosity by the powers from "on high." The poor were not particularly respected for their simple state; they were merely the lucky recipients of the kind and beneficent rich. Lamps were placed in front of tabernacles in the early days of the thirteenth century to prevent street crime, which was rampant. Florence at that time was the scene of violent family vendettas as well as constant brawls between non-Christians and Christians. An ingenious solution was devised to finance the oil lamps of the tabernacles: for five years after their release from prison, pardoned criminals were given the responsibility of buying the oil and keeping the lamps in working order. These tabernacle oil lamps were the only source of street illumination until 1783, when public light fixtures were installed around the city. Nowadays the storekeeper from the stationery shop across the street provides fresh flowers every other day for the shrine.

Turn right onto via de' Pucci. The sixteenth-century Pucci Palace, at nos. 2–4, looms over almost the whole street on your left. The Puccis were upstanding members of the nobility descended from a thirteenth-century carpenter of some literary fame. The Pucci Palace was renovated in the seventeenth century; the outside and many details inside the courtyard have remained the same. The Pucci coat of arms over the main door is intriguing: the stone-carved Moorish gentleman's head shows the artistic influence of the Moorish and Tartar slaves who filled the grand palaces of Florence.

Walk inside the front door. The entire ground floor of the palace has been turned into a subdued mini-shopping mall of shoe stores, a beauty parlor, and business offices. Directly to the left of the door is a pleasant secondhand bookstore, Istituto Studi Etruschi. The bookstore owner is friendly, speaks English, and is especially knowledgeable about nineteenth-century books.

Tabernacle of the Five Lamps (via de' Ricasoli and via de' Pucci)

Medieval-looking lamps with delicately inscribed paper shades are the "signs" posted in front of each shop.

Outside the palace, at no. 4, is the modestly priced restaurant, Le Cantine. The entrance is under one of the palace windows and behind a small wooden door.

Walk to the end of the palace where via de' Pucci meets via de' Servi. Cross the street to your right and stand or sit on the steps of the small church of San Michelino Visdomini. You'll be facing the rough-stoned corner of the Pucci Palace with the fleur-de-lis coat of arms between the first and second floors. Notice the cemented lower window on the first floor. The Florentines have a story to explain this mystery. Puccio Pucci, a fourteenth-century kinsman, in cahoots with Cosimo de' Medici started to pile up the family fortune. By the sixteenth century, however, one Pandolfo Pucci was thrown out of the court by Cosimo I. Offended by his social blackballing, Pandolfo decided to station himself in the windows of the Pucci Palace on the corner of via de' Servi and take potshots at Cosimo on his way to some festivities at the Church of SS. Annunziata. Cosimo survived but Pandolfo was arrested and hanged from the windows of the Bargello. Fifteen years later, Orazio Pucci, in an effort to vindicate the family name, entered into another, similar conspiracy. He was caught and hanged from the same Bargello windows. Cosimo decided that the corner window of this palace should no longer serve as a shooting gallery and he ordered it permanently closed.

The house across from the Pucci Palace and to your left was the home of the first Jewish Medici. Rabbi Jochiel was a highly respected sixteenth-century physician, and was the family doctor of the Medicis. When the rabbi decided to convert to Catholicism, no less a personage than Pope Gregory XIII baptized him, and Cardinal Medici was his godfather. After the ceremony, he was officially granted the name of Medici and his sons continued to carry on a new line of the Florentine dynasty. The Medici coat of arms hangs over the corner of the building.

The cross street via de' Servi most likely derives its name from one of the two following sources. One account has it that this street was named for the servants of the Church of SS. Annunziata just down the road. Another version claims that the name is derived from runaway slaves and maidservants who once populated the neighborhood.

From the steps of the church, walk to your right and down via Bufalini. This street was named for a celebrated nineteenth-century doctor who lived on this block.

At the end of via Bufalini, where it meets with via Sant'Egidio, is a large open space to your left. The building behind this piazza is the Hospital of Santa Maria Nuova. A thirteenth-century hospital was once situated here; it was founded by Folco Portinari, the father of Dante's beloved Beatrice. Folco first thought of building a hospital when his woman servant, Madonna Tessa, started bringing sick people in off the streets into the house. In 1285, Folco decided to move the hospital ward out of his home. Medieval hospices and hospitals were usually located near or outside the city gates; travelers were housed, fed, and cared for there free of charge. In the thirteenth century, the city wall cut through the intersection of via de' Pucci and via de' Servi. Folco built his hospital on a spot that was about 125 yards outside the city wall. The hospital that you see now was put up in the fourteenth century. Buontalenti, a celebrated sixteenth-century architect, designed the upper-story loggia and façade of the hospital; in the eighteenth century the top floor was added.

Walk inside the hospital door marked no. 1. You're now entering the oldest part of the hospital, the fourteenth-century courtyard. A few feet inside and to your right is a striking marble bas-relief of Monna Tessa, Portinari's servant. The sculpture is dated 1288, the year of her death. A covered terrace that looks like the entrance to a Greek temple is the focal point of the courtyard. Statues of illustrious Florentines decorate the walls of the terrace. The marble monument in the center is of Count Galli-Tassi, a generous benefactor who left his entire fortune to the hospital.

Have a seat on one of the walls or steps along the courtyard if you're in need of shade or relaxation.

In the fourteenth century, Santa Maria Nuova served a variety of charitable services. The sick and elderly were tended to, and the poor were given money and food. Most conspicuous of all the activities carried out here were the care and raising of Florence's burgeoning population of illegitimate children. With the in-

Fourteenth-century courtyard of Hospital of Santa Maria Nuova

crease of wealth due to the prospering textile industry, the demand for household servants and slaves in Florence also increased. These additions to the family circle created new bonds, and the results of the bonds were hundreds of foundlings, children who went unacknowledged by their fathers and uncared for by their mothers. Santa Maria Nuova took in the foundlings. When, in the fifteenth century, there was no longer enough room for them here, a new refuge, the Spedale degli Innocenti ("Hospital of the Innocents"), was built a few blocks away in Piazza SS. Annunziata. The foundlings, along with the other patients at Santa Maria Nuova, were looked after by members of the clergy. The *spedalingo*, or "warden," was a priest. The male and female nurses were sworn to poverty and chastity. Throughout the fourteenth century, the hospital was supported by donations from some of the wealthy patriarchs who contributed to the foundling population in Florence. Santa Maria Nuova was remembered in many a last will and testament, and probably because of not a few guilty consciences. By the early fifteenth century the hospital was in possession of over fifty lucrative farms, vineyards, and estates, and the produce and rent from these properties added considerably to the coffers of this much-needed charitable institution.

Walk back outside the courtyard, cross the parking lot, and head down the street directly opposite the hospital's front door, via Folco Portinari.

Three-quarters of the way down the street, on your right, at no. 11/r, is a sleek glass and white-walled wool shop. Skeins of every hue in the rainbow are stacked like logs along the open windows and inside shelves of the shop. The hours are generally evening ones, from 7:00 to 9:00 P.M.

Turn left onto via dell'Oriuolo. This street is short on history (for a change) but long on shade in the summer. There is an exotic sculpture garden, and several unconventional stores to browse around in.

The first clock for the tower of the Palazzo Vecchio was built on this street in 1353. The name of the street became via dell'Oriuolo, a variation on *orologio*, which means "watch" or "clock."

At no. 31 is the Teatro dell'Oriuolo. Three different theater companies alternately put on productions here, and you can buy tickets at the box office. All performances are in Italian.

The promised sculpture garden is on the left side of the street at no. 24. Once the garden of the fifteenth-century convent that's behind the trees and artwork, it's now a twentieth-century oasis for reading and relaxing. A constantly changing exhibit of contemporary sculpture is scattered around the lawn and inside the open porch of what was the convent. The garden is open from 9:00 A.M. to 7:00 P.M. every day; on Sundays it's open from 9:00 A.M. to 1:00 P.M.; it's closed every Thursday. Inside the convent are two museums: the Historical Museum of Topography, Museo di Firenze com'era, (roughly translatable as "Florence as it was"), which is open from 10:00 A.M. to 2:00 P.M. on weekdays and 9:00 A.M. to 12:00 noon on Sundays and closed Thursdays; and the Florentine Museum of Prehistory (Museo Fiorentino di Preistoria), which is open every day from 9:30 A.M. to 12:30 but closed on Mondays.

The Historical Museum of Topography is small, casual, and a welcome relief from grandiose palaces and wall-to-wall Old Masters. The walls of this museum are filled with old maps, etchings, photographs, and paintings of Florence that date back to the fifteenth century. Any dedicated Florencewalker will also recognize some half-dozen historical views of streets covered in this book.

Cross the street and look for no. 17. This is the family palace of the Albizi clan, upstanding members of the Guelph party and arch-rivals of the Medici for political control of Florence during the fourteenth century. The Medici finally took over Florence in 1433 after both families had murdered and exiled each other for decades. The fourteenth-century home extends all the way back to Borgo degli Albizi, a cross street that we'll pass shortly. Stroll inside the courtyard, once a luxurious garden and now a parking lot. One flourishing palm tree is left as a reminder of the Albizi stronghold.

At no. 31/r is another shop that is one-of-a-kind in Florence: Casa del Fumetto, "The Comic Book House." In Italian, the word for comic book, *fumetto*, comes from *fumo*, or "smoke." The balloon-bordered words that come out of the mouths of comic book characters look like puffs of smoke; hence comic books are *fumetti*, "things of smoke."

The Comic Book House is a family-run business. One tiny toom is crammed with albums and cartons and files of old Italian postcards, calendars, photographs, advertisements, and books on such topics as Imperial Chinese ceramics and American movie producers of the 1930s. The most popular items in the store by far are the "Topolino" (Italian Mickey Mouse) comic books. Superman comics, in Italian, run a close second. Opera librettos, old portrait photographs, and pictures of Florentine street scenes are also for sale.

Cross the street and continue walking down the left side of via dell'Oriuolo and stop at no. 34/r. You'll never see a shop window—or a shop—quite like this one again: dressed-up dolls and puppets and stuffed animals lounge around the corners of the window as if they are digesting a particularly huge picnic. Along the ledges of the windowpane are rows and rows of blue and green and gray glass eyeballs. Walk inside the door and against the wall to your right will be bunches of plastic arms and legs hanging from hooks like banana plants. Perched on shelves and cabinets all over

the room are severed doll heads, worn-out mario-
nettes, and a cluster of porcelain Madonna figures in
need of medical attention. This is Fontana, the only remaining doll hospital in Florence. The owner, Ottavio
Fontana, has performed restorative miracles in this
shop for over forty years. When asked exactly how
long he had been repairing puppets, dolls, manne-
quins, and religious statues, he shrugged his shoulders
and said, *"Da cent'anni"* ("For a hundred years"). Signor Fontana began working as a clerk in a store when
he was very young. Whenever something broke, it was
his job to fix it. He discovered that his talent in life was
working with his hands and repairing objects; in Florence his talent is an appreciated and recognized art.
Florentines will go to extreme lengths to repair a
chipped tool, a worn sweater, or a faulty doorknob before considering replacing it. This isn't a sign of miser-
liness, but rather a respect for an artisan's work. Signor
Fontana's favorite patients at the doll hospital are theater puppets. He loves to touch up or repaint their
faces. His least favorite invalids are modern plastic
dolls: "They're much harder to repair because they
have more parts."

Visitors are always welcome to watch Signor Fontana or one of his colleagues spray-paint new skin
tones on a doll or stitch away at an embroidered gar-
ment. There's a small tin box on his desk in the front
of the shop. Any visitor can make a small donation
of a hundred lire or so to Signor Fontana's religious
charity.

Walk all the way to the end of via dell'Oriuolo and
stop in the open square where it converges with four
other streets. On the extreme left is via Sant'Egidio,
which looks almost like an extension of via dell'
Oriuolo. A pottery shop, Sbigoli Terrecotte, is on the
corner of via Sant'Egidio (4/r) and Borgo Pinti. Their
plates, pitchers, and tiles are shipped all over the
world, and American Express and BankAmericard are
familiar forms of payment here.

A display of seltzer bottles and wine carafes
stands—sometimes—behind a glass window show-
case on the corner building of Borgo Pinti. This is a
decoration of sorts put up by the adjoining restaurant,
Da Cosimo, at via dell'Oriuolo 16/r and Borgo Pinti
4/r. The prices in this trattoria are low, the food is well

prepared, and the dining rooms are enhanced by old lamps, antiques, and original oil paintings.

Take a short detour down the medieval street of Borgo Pinti. A few doors to the left of the trattoria is the small artisans' workshop and store I Maschereri ("The Mask Makers") at Borgo Pinti 18/r. Set designs, props, and theater masks are produced in the back of the large studio. Dozens of gilded, ebony, and chalk-white masks are on display and for sale in the front area. Prices for these theater masks range from $20 to $45.

The artisans of this shop have a special interest in preserving the character of the original masks of the sixteenth-century theatrical company *commedia dell' arte*, but they've added their own nuances and artistic interpretations to the papier-mâché and leather creations. I Masquereri was the name of the sixteenth-century guild of maskmakers that was especially established by the "commedia dell'arte." Maskmaking and papier-mâché work is a dying art in Italy. Until World War II a small band of Florentine craftsmen created a unique breed of dolls made entirely of papier-mâché; and some small towns in Tuscany still maintain the maskmaking tradition for yearly carnivals, but the demand is limited. The nearby city of Viareggio on the northwestern coast of Tuscany enjoyed a recent surge of papier-mâché-making activity when movie director Federico Fellini ordered scores of extravagant floats with larger-than-life-size movable figures for his epic film *Casanova*.

Our walk will resume back at the juncture of Borgo Pinti and via dell'Oriuolo. Look for the dark *volta*, or "archway," that's directly ahead as you come out of Borgo Pinti. In the summer, flower vendors are stationed directly under the via dell'Oriuolo side of the arch. This medieval *volta* was an architectural link built to connect two neighboring houses that belonged to the same clan. The *volte* also served as dramatic entranceways into a family's geographic "territory," in this case the powerful Albizi, long-standing enemies of the Medici. The rooms inside the arch were once used as storage space by the merchants whose wares were sold in the old marketplace that we're about to enter. In the nineteenth century shopkeepers took over the warehouses. This archway is one of the very few left in Florence that are still used for commercial purposes.

To your right inside the *volta* is the store Dean at no. 9/r. Expensive costume jewelry and porcelain-faced puppets are the standard fare. The unusual offerings in this shop are the brass reproductions of medieval votives, amply displayed in the window. Centuries ago the original baubles were purchased to ward off infectious diseases that afflicted both man and beast. Whatever the ailment, there was a silver- or gold-plated replica of the appropriate anatomical part that could be purchased and appealed to in prayer. The brass copies that you see in the window will give you an idea of the surrealistic appearance of the medieval prototypes. Six-inch to one-foot-high arms and legs, mouths and necks, eyes and chests, cows, horses, sheep, swaddled babies, and breasts are all for sale in the $10 to $12 price range. The original antique votives are collector's items.

Walk out of the archway and into the bright light of Piazza San Pier Maggiore. On the left side of the piazza is a large arched wall that faces Borgo degli Albizi. A very old church, from the twelfth or thirteenth century, once stood behind the arch, which was built by the Albizi family in 1638. The Albizi family emblem is carved along the top of the wall; it somewhat resembles an eyeball with two arched eyebrows above it.

The now-missing Church of San Pier Maggiore was the medieval location for the installation of the Bishop of Florence. A curious "wedding" ceremony took place for the occasion: the newly appointed bishop arrived at the church, dressed to the teeth and accompanied by a retinue of clerical officials. The abbess of the nearby Benedictine convent then appeared, escorted by a bevy of nuns. The priest of San Pier Maggiore performed a mock wedding ceremony and the new bishop presented the abbess with a wedding ring! After a great deal of feasting on everyone's part, the bishop then retired for the night, presumably alone, at the parish house. The next day the clerical leader and his companions appeared in the piazza, ceremoniously removed their shoes and walked barefoot back to the Duomo by way of Borgo degli Albizi.

The open space in front of the seventeenth-century wall, now known as Piazza San Pier Maggiore, is an ex-

Archway of San Pier Maggiore

ample of accidental town planning in the Middle Ages. Churches at that time were always set back a little from the row of houses and other public buildings that rose along the street. This space separation eventually took on a sacred character because of its association with the adjoining church. But nothing in medieval Florence was so sacred that some money could not be exchanged over it. The parish church of every neighborhood was the center for the legalization of all commercial and social contracts. Financial discussions and business arrangements also spilled out onto the hallowed ground in front of the church. Soon moneylenders and merchants with booths and tables full of merchandise were a common sight. A medieval business complex formed on the open space in front of the parish church.

Piazza San Pier Maggiore was also just inside one of the principal gates to the town, and throughout medieval and Renaissance days it was one of the busiest zones of commerce in Florence. The piazza is still an active trade thoroughfare. In morning hours you'll see an array of vegetable stands set up for business around the great wall of the old Albizi family compound.

The next street on our walk is via Matteo Palmieri, which, if you're facing the Albizi wall, is to your right. Palmieri was a fifteenth-century pharmacist and an extremely influential man of letters. His pharmacy is still in business after five hundred years, but modern medicine has replaced the original Renaissance stock of potions and herbs. If you're in the mood for a short detour, walk around the left side of the wall and continue about 100 yards down to the corner of via dell' Oriuolo and via Fiesolana. There, facing you squarely, at no. 83/r, is a fifteenth-century building with a pale orange awning over the front door. This is Palmieri's Farmacia del Canto alle Rondini, the "Pharmacy of the Swallows' Corner." Palmieri's store is located in a section of the neighborhood once owned by another strong clan, the Donati, whose medieval tower we'll stop in front of in a few minutes. The Donati coat of arms consisted of three swallows flying against a gold background, and this part of their property was always referred to as "The Swallows' Corner."

If you took the detour, amble back to Piazza San Pier Maggiore.

Read a page or so ahead about Palmieri before continuing down this street, which is named for him.

In the mid-1430s the literary pharmacist wrote a book entitled *Della Vita Civile* (*On Civic Life*), and because of this treatise he was instrumental in easing the guilt feelings of well-to-do Florentines who were eager to make and spend more money. All during the Middle Ages and up until that period the prevailing attitude toward wealth was that it was all right to make it but not to flaunt it. Palmieri himself came from a modest background and, as his wealth increased, he learned to cultivate the fine art of enjoying one's fortune. Palmieri assured the fifteenth-century Florentines that being successful and showing it was a form of civic pride and an inspiration to all. As a result, the rich and conscientious citizens of Florence began to take his words to heart. Lavish costumery came into fashion and stately, extravagantly built palazzos were the new norm in housing. Florentine matrons suddenly abandoned the drab clothes and discreet behavior of the stodgy medieval days and plunged into a fashion-conscious fling in the mid-fifteenth century. A contemporary but anonymous admirer of the Florentine female toilette wrote:

> Was there ever save for them a painter, nay even a mere dyer, who could turn black into white? Certainly not; for it is against nature. Yet, if a face is yellow and pallid, they change it by artificial means to the hue of a rose. One who, by nature or age, has a skinny figure, they are able to make florid and plump. I do not think Giotto or any other painter could colour better than they do; but the most wonderful thing is, that even a face which is out of proportion, and has goggle eyes, they will make correct with eyes like to a falcon's. As to crooked noses, they are soon put straight. If they have jaws like a donkey, they quickly correct them. If their shoulders are too large, they plane them; if one projects more than the other, they stuff them so with cotton that they seem in proportion.

Walk a few feet down via Matteo Palmieri, past the two sidewalk trattorias and stop at no. 35/r. This is the five-story medieval tower of the Donati family.

At least one generation of Donatis is legendary for being hot-blooded and headstrong. Corso Donati, in the thirteenth century, literally got away with murder, and his sister Piccarda went to her grave before passing a night in the connubial state.

Toward the end of the thirteenth century, when the Guelph party ruled Florence, Guelph party members began to get restless and started fighting with each other. The political situation became so chaotic that Guelph families split into various factions and battled it out with each other whenever an occasion to do so arose.

One day in deep December of 1294, Corso Donati met up with a rival cousin, Simone, and his groom in the streets of Florence. An argument ensued; Simone was injured, his groom was killed, and the case came to court. Corso was a smooth talker and he presented his case so convincingly that the *podestà*, or "judge," ruled that Simone, rather than Corso, should be condemned to death for the murder of his groom. On January 25, 1295, the judge's sentence was made public. No sooner were the words out of the bailiff's mouth than a mob rallied in the streets and rushed over to the judge's house. At the sight of the discontented constituents, the judge dashed to the roof, climbed over various neighbors' roofs, and found some kind of haven until the incident blew over. Meanwhile, the crowd broke open the doors of the judge's house and stormed through the rooms destroying everything in sight. A few days later, the judge made his way back to his chambers and revoked his sentence on the cousin. Corso was let off with a modest fine for his crime.

Piccarda Donati, on the other hand, did not fare as well in life as her brother. Famed for her beauty and, probably even more impressive, her dowry, Piccarda was engaged, very much against her will, to one Rossellino della Tosa. On the eve before her wedding, Piccarda made off to a convent that was only a few blocks down from the Donati tower. She hastily took the veil the next morning and renamed herself "Sister Constanza." Her father, brother Corso, and provoked fiancé discovered her whereabouts; and they carried the irate nun home and informed her of her marital obligations: she was to be wed the next day, and a guard was placed in front of her bedroom door. That night, while praying in front of her crucifix, Piccarda started to itch and moan. Tiny white worms appeared all over her limbs. By morning, Piccarda had died, still a nun in body and in spirit.

Gemma Donati, a cousin of Corso and Piccarda, married the poet Dante.

Continue walking down via Palmieri. This very old road was once known as via del Mercatino, or "Street of the Little Market." Notice the small artisans' shops along the way that are now converted into jewelry and craft stores. One remaining studio is at no. 26/r on the left side of the street. This is a mattress-makers' workshop where a constantly rotating multi-generational crew is always at work stuffing and stitching and binding.

Cross via de' Pandolfini. A few doors down from the mattress workshop at nos. 16/r–14/r is Salimbeni, the largest and best-stocked art bookstore in Florence. Architectural books, urban planning tracts, portfolios of prints, and artists' memoirs can be found on the shelves and tables. The sales help is particular (for good reason) about how visitors handle the books. When you're perusing a $200 volume on Italian villas, make sure that the book binding is resting securely on a hard surface or you'll get a gentle reprimanding from the staff. You can spend unlimited hours steeped in Salimbeni's selections. The Salimbeni were a famous Sienese family in Renaissance days. The motto of the family was *Per non dormire*, "Not to sleep," which is also a fitting enough motto for bookstore owners.

Via Palmieri turns into via dell'Isola delle Stinche at the intersection with via Ghibellina. The street was named "Island of the Stinche" because a prison, the "Stinche," once stood directly on your left where the block-long, white-walled Teatro Verdi now sits. This prison was built in 1299 for aristocratic inmates only. Among the clientele were Giovanni Villani, who filled his idle moments by writing *The Chronicles of Florence*, and Giovanni Cavalcante, a nabob of the nobility and a contemporary of Dante. The name "Stinche" was bestowed on the establishment because in 1304 the Cavalcantis themselves were attacked by a feuding neighborhood militia in their country house, the Castle of Stinche. The Cavalcantis successfully defended their home, captured a few dozen enemy soldiers, and sent them off to the Florentine prison. By the fifteenth century, the "Stinche" became more democratic in its acceptance of prisoners and virtually anyone, regardless of social position, could be incarcerated here. Bankruptcy was the most common offense of the inmates. The "Stinche" was torn down in 1838; the theater was built then.

The small side street between the theater and the parish church facing S. Simone piazza at the end of the street is called via dei Lavatoi. Wool-washing workrooms once lined this street in the textile industry's Renaissance heyday in Florence. The district surrounding and to the west of Piazza Santa Croce was the working-class suburb of wool and silk businesses. The dyeing, rinsing, stretching, and drying of fabric was a messy, smelly activity. The damp and noisy workshops and workers' homes were confined to neighborhoods

Thirteenth-century Salviati Palace with sporti *additions to the upper floors*

far from the elegant center of Florence so as not to offend the upper classes. Other textile work areas were located along the banks of the Arno, where the soap and dyes could easily be drained into the flowing waters.

Before walking into Piazza San Simone stop at the corner of via della Vigna Vecchia, the "Street of the Old Vineyard," which is on your right. Medieval priests once tended a sizable grape crop here. The street's name was meant to distinguish it from another road on the western side of Florence, via della Vigna Nuova, the "Street of the New Vineyard."

On the corner of via della Vigna Vecchia and via dell'Isola delle Stinche at nos. 19–23/r is the thirteenth-century palace of the Salviati family. (A used-furniture store is on the ground level of the palace.) The Salviatis, along with the Albizis and Donatis, were long-standing political rivals of the Medicis. Notice how many Medici enemies are geographically clustered on this side of Florence.

The Salviati Palace is an architectural landmark, and worth a few minutes' inspection. The outside walls of the palace above ground level jut out or "project" into the street. These projections of the wall surface are called *sporti*. We saw (pages 52–53) how tower dwellers were able to set up and remove wooden balconies on the outside walls of their homes; brackets on the balconies were hooked into holes in the tower walls. A later architectural feature stemmed from this: some towers in Florence began to be built with stone and brick projections on the top floor in imitation of the old wooden balconies. (See the top section of the Palazzo Vecchio for this effect.) Florentines also enlarged their living space by building the same stone and brick projections along the inside walls in a family compound of towers that faced an interior courtyard.

In 1250 a law was passed to limit the height of towers. The Florentines decided to build laterally as much as space would permit. *Sporti* of brick, stone, and half-timber were added onto the second floor of homes; and the extensions continued all the way up to the roof. Throughout the fourteenth and fifteenth centuries, the Florentines continued to "project" their walls toward the street until, in 1533, the building of *sporti* was decreed unsafe and illegal. Buildings with completely flat façades then became the new architectural style.

Walk over to the Church of San Simone in the left corner of the piazza in front of you. Built in 1202, it was a fancier replacement for the tiny chapel that once stood here in the midst of the monks' garden of grapevines. San Simone became a parish church to the neighborhood in 1293. On February 14, 1551, a band of women suspected of heresy were burned to death in the center of Piazza San Simone.

The church was redecorated at the end of the seventeenth century by Silvani, one of Florence's most sought-after architects. He also renovated the fifteenth-century interior of the much grander Church of San Marco in Piazza San Marco. The church is often closed during the day but the doors are always opened shortly before the 6:00 P.M. mass. Take a look inside if you have wandered by at an opportune time. The interior is surprisingly colorful, with a gold-leaf ceiling and brightly painted canvases of reds, pinks, and blues.

Across the street from the church, at no. 7/r, is one of Florence's gustatory landmarks: Vivoli's, a world-famous watering hole for the ice cream epicurean. O1 warm days and evenings the entire piazza, including the steps of San Simone, is crowded with Vivoli's customers, scooping and spooning away at Dixie cups full of banana, mousse, almond, and rum concoctions.

The ice cream parlor is oddly decorated. A neon sign over the counter glares out in saucy Italian: ". . . *e tutti vengono qui d'ogni paese, lor desiando lo gelatomio* . . ." which means ". . . and everyone comes from different nations to eat *my ice cream* . . ." Vivoli's prides itself on sending 50 kilos of ice cream a week to Switzerland and, in the summer months, to some New York ice cream parlors. The walls of the store are covered with photographs autographed by international soccer and crew teams, race car drivers, movie stars, and musicians who've enjoyed a stop at Vivoli's. A few tables and a wall-long, fish-filled aquarium are in a back alcove. Take note of the public bathroom, a Florentine rarity.

If good ice cream makes you homesick, you might want to stroll across the piazza and take in a movie at the Astro Cinema, directly to the right of the church. All movies are in English, and the theater is open every night except Monday.

The jewelry shop next door to the theater, at no. 2/r, is of the handcrafted, mixed-media style. Loopy gold earrings, plastic-beaded necklaces, and feather-twined bracelets are the stock here. The young jewelry craftspeople also double as the sales help. There's not a great deal of English spoken in the shop, but everyone is helpful and friendly.

Continue walking 15 yards beyond Vivoli's, and stop on your right at the narrow via delle Burelle. In Roman days, when Christian martyrs were regularly flung to lions in the amphitheater across the road, this small alleyway served as the residence for the hungry animals. (We'll be walking along the curve of the old amphitheater soon.) For many centuries after leonine amusements were out of fashion, these lions' dens remained in operation. The compartments were used from time to time to house surplus prisoners or criminals. Such an emergency usually occurred after a successful battle with neighboring hillside towns. In Dante's day, more than 740 political prisoners were detained in the Roman lions' dens.

Across from via delle Burelle is via Torta, one of the winding medieval streets that follow the perimeter of the old Roman amphitheater. Turn left and walk down via Torta. A popular restaurant whose name recalls former amphitheater amusements is at no. 7/r: Leo in Santa Croce. At the end of the twisting via Torta looms the thirteenth-century marble-faced Church of Santa Croce.

The palace around the corner and to the right of the restaurant is the Palazzo Serristori (sometimes referred to as the Palazzo Cocchi). The palace is drab-looking today but the address is, and always has been, prestigious—no. 1 Piazza Santa Croce. The view of the church from the living-room windows has to be an impressive sight. Designed and built in the sixteenth century by Baccio d'Agnolo, the residence has always boasted a classy group of tenants. Most of the inhabitants have also ended up, postmortemly speaking, across the street in the church encased in an elegant family chapel. The eighteenth-century resident of the palace was Antonio Cocchi, a physician, historical linguist, connoisseur of antiques, and companion of Sir Isaac Newton. Cocchi is buried in Santa Croce under a marble likeness of himself.

Napoleon Bonaparte's brother, Joseph, who liked to be called the Count of Surviller, moved into the palace in the early nineteenth century. The count and his wife, mysteriously referred to as "Mme Clary," and their daughter lived a relatively quiet life for socialite Florentines at the time. Guido Biagi, head of the Laurentian Library and historian of Florentine social mores, wrote of the count's activities in the palace:

> . . . he gave sumptuous dinners, but no grand balls or receptions, as Mme Clary was in weak health.

(She is now permanently confined to the Bonaparte Chapel across the street.)

> He protected the arts, patronized artists, and went every day to the Cascine [the extensive public park in Florence] in a large "calèche" with eight springs, the body and the coach-box being straw-coloured, like all the equipages of the Bonapartes.

Biagi also mentions that the entire Bonaparte brood was particularly fond of this palace and tended to rendezvous here in the evenings for brandy and card-playing.

Walk to the palace's other corner, and go all the way down the street that's to the left and behind the palace, via dell'Anguillara; continue past the small antique shops along this street.

Stop at the corner of via dell'Anguillara and the curving via Bentaccordi. The name of this street is a pun on its peculiar shape; *bentaccordi* means the "bent tail of a dog."

After turning left down this street, pause a few steps down next to the house that's on your right. A plaque on the wall tells you that this is the boyhood home of Michelangelo Buonarroti, who lived here when he was approximately between the ages of six and fourteen. At the time that the old Florentine family of Buonarroti was living here their ancestral fortune had dwindled and left them slightly above poverty level. Michelangelo's father, Lodovico, had sold off all the family farms except one in nearby Settignano, and in the mid-1480s had moved his clan of a half-dozen children, wife, and servants to the city. Without even a Buonarroti palace to his name, Lodovico was forced to rent this house from his brother-in-law, a prosperous wool-dyer.

When Michelangelo entered adolescence and came of wage-earning age, he decided that he wanted no part of the business life in Florence. His father was ready to apprentice him to the Wool Guild; Michelangelo wanted to be an artist. Numerous fights, entreaties, and tantrums took place behind these walls while father and son attempted to come to an agreement about the fate of the Buonarroti name. Lodovico, like many men of his time, considered artists to be little more than laborers. Meanwhile, Michelangelo had gone around to Domenico Ghirlandaio's studio and done the unheard of: he asked the old master to pay *him* to be an apprentice in his fresco business (it was always the other way around, with the young man's family contributing to the teacher's income until the student had learned the trade). Ghirlandaio looked over some of Michelangelo's drawings and agreed to the unorthodox arrangement. The young Buonarroti ran home to tell his father of the extra florins that would be coming in from the artist's studio, and Lodovico grudgingly gave his consent to the new career.

Michelangelo began his apprenticeship as a fresco painter, and he proved to be a model student in every way except when it came to getting along with his fellow workers. He was always ready to pick a fight with the other apprentices, and Ghirlandaio, who was known for his patience and kindness, soon ran out of these virtues with the stubborn and arrogant young Michelangelo. When Lorenzo ("Il Magnifico") de' Medici decided to open a sculptors' school in a garden near Piazza San Marco, he asked Ghirlandaio to nominate one of his students for enrollment. Ghirlandaio wasted no time in suggesting the unruly Michelangelo. So the young fresco apprentice was forced to make an unexpected career change.

One day while he was busily chipping and chiseling away in the garden, Michelangelo turned and saw the Medici prince watching him intently. Lorenzo knew talent when he saw it, and he asked Michelangelo if he wanted to come over and live at the Medici Palace. The sculptor replied that his father would have to agree first. "Il Magnifico" sent a messenger over to via Bentaccordi with a summons for Lodovico to appear at the palace. The unsuspecting Lodovico walked over to via Cavour and was shown into the royal chambers. There Lorenzo asked him whether Michelangelo could come and live with him as a son. The older Buonarroti readily agreed, realizing that, after all, it was one less mouth to feed. As a parting gesture, the prince asked the impoverished aristocrat if there were any jobs around Florence that he wanted. Lodovico thought a moment and said that he might like a steady income as a customs accountant. This was easily arranged, and the Buonarroti of via Bentaccordi began to see better times. The astonished father started to enjoy a weekly paycheck, and his wayward son moved over to the Medici Palace and started his life as a prince of the art world.

As you turn left and proceed down via Bentaccordi, look down along both sides of the street: 2½-feet-tall stone strips are mounted against the walls of the houses. These vertical curbstones were placed along via Bentaccordi to protect the walls from the scrape of carriage wheels as they made the sharp turns through this narrow lane.

To the right of the street, at no. 1, you'll see a small

wooden door. This was the entrance for beggars to stand by and hope for the best in food disposal from the palace kitchen.

About 35 yards from via dell'Anguillara is the next cross street, Borgo dei Greci. In 1439 Pope Eugenius IV called together a council of the Greek and Latin churches in a spirit of ecclesiastical unification. Unofficial sources claim that the patriarch of the Greek Church, along with his brother, the emperor of Byzantium, were put up in the palaces along this street for the convention; hence, the name "Borgo of the Greeks."

Another 20 yards ahead via Bentaccordi makes an abrupt swing to the left; you'll find yourself in Piazza de' Peruzzi. The original site of the family loggia was in front of the green-shuttered two-story house that you'll spot as soon as you come out of via Bentaccordi. Here, the Peruzzi banking potentates discussed business matters of the highest order. In 1339, the Peruzzi family was in a position to make an enormous loan to the King of England. When the Royal Crown defaulted on the loan, the Peruzzi and most of the working population of Florence were ruined. The merchant class, which had invested heavily in the loan, lost its working capital, and the working class, made up of artisans, dyers, and weavers, lost many jobs. The Peruzzi, who had negotiated the loan through their bank, wisely left town for a few decades and later returned to live a low-profile existence for the next few centuries. They managed to recoup some of their financial losses and become politically active again in the nineteenth century during the political movement to unify all of Italy.

Ubaldino Peruzzi, in this later period, was a popular man-about-town and mayor of Florence. E. Grifi, the local Florentine historian, relates an interesting sartorial detail about His Honor:

> His figure was a friendly one to each Florentine; and for that disposition of kindly humor that marks the people of Florence even in the most serious events and in its dearest affections; among the Florentines still exists the remembrance of his trousers which he used to wear too short by several inches. Even now trousers of less than conventional length are called alla Peruzzi.

* * *

The old Peruzzi palaces turn all the way down the left side of the street following the curve of the old amphitheater. At the end of the block is the dramatic stone Peruzzi Arch, the fourteenth-century entrance to the family territory.

Walk back to the junction of via Bentaccordi and the Piazza de' Peruzzi.

To the right of via Bentaccordi and of the piazza is via de' Rustici, the next street along our walk. Stop about 3 feet away from the piazza at no. 25. Look to the upper right of this house and you'll see the carved stone plaque of a serenely posed saint. This bas-relief seems to have been "borrowed" from an old church or tomb and reinstalled on the housefront. Another few feet ahead, at no. 7, is a wooden door. In the left corner of this entrance, imbedded in the wall, is a jewel of a polychromed tile with the Madonna and Child.

The street stones along via de' Rustici are very old, probably dating from the Middle Ages. The Romans used polygonally-cut stones such as these for road paving but via de' Rustici was never part of the Roman town. The square-shaped stones along the sidewalk are newer.

At no. 5 is the distinguished Florentine publishing house Edizioni Bonechi.

Fifty yards from the start of via de' Rustici and to your right is the back wall of the eleventh-century parish Church of San Remigio. Architecturally, the tiny church is unique because of the pointed belltower that rises up over via de' Rustici. The church's belltower, or *campanile*, is an architectural hybrid—a medieval tower turned into a Late Middle Ages religious structure.

In the tower-building boom of eleventh-century Florence, many large clans constructed several adjoining towers that formed fortresslike family compounds. One of the towers would become the chapel and living quarters for the priest. But in these early days of medieval Christianity, a more important use of the tower-church was as a general meeting place for family and friendly neighbors. A bell, or *campana*, was placed on the top floor of the tower. Whenever a political or social meeting was scheduled, or an emergency came up, the bell in the church tower would be rung and the family members and allies would come scurrying.

In the later days of the Middle Ages, bell towers were built exactly like medieval resident towers. They were either stuck onto the sides of churches or they became entirely separate structures a few yards away from the church. Giotto's fourteenth-century *campanile* in Piazza del Duomo is a highly spruced-up later edition of the earlier, more modest family-compound bell tower. The Church of San Remigio is unusual because the *campanile* is not a distinct or separate feature from the church; it still resembles an eleventh-century medieval tower.

Walk around to the right of the church through via Vinegia and go inside the main entrance.

The priest of San Remigio believes that an even older church dating from the ninth century was on this spot. He also has a hunch that the slender Romanesque windows at the sides of the building were from this earlier church. The eleventh-century parish was enlarged in the 1300s, and the church was redecorated in the Gothic style that you see now. The only change is that the altar was in the middle of the room. When seventeenth-century Baroque taste effloresced in Florence, the interior of San Remigio's was coated with gilt, glitter, and garniture. Rows of altars were placed around the side of the church. When the flood of the Arno in 1966 stained and mangled the Baroque decor, the tiny church was cleaned up and restored to its thirteenth-century parish appearance.

A seal of the Medici family is on the first pilaster against the wall to the left of the main entrance. Frescoes from the thirteenth century peer out of the semi-darkness along the stone walls. Walk over to the left wall facing the altar and you'll discover a luminous pastel tile of a shaggy dog gleefully jumping out of a wine barrel. The priest thinks that the tile was donated by a Renaissance wine-making family who lived in the neighborhood—perhaps in the side street, via Vinegia.

Over the centuries most of San Remigio's artwork has been sold. "The church is practically bare of Madonnas," the priest remarked regretfully one day as he walked up the aisle to mid-afternoon mass.

When you're outside the church again, you'll notice

Wall tile inside the Church of San Remigio

holes scattered around the exterior stone walls. This is where the medieval scaffolding was fitted when construction was being carried out.

The horizontal lintels over the large and smaller doors of the church are made of a massive and costly stone called *pietra serena* ("clear stone"), which is found on the hillsides outside of Florence. The smaller pieces around the arches of the doorways are made of a tannish stone that fractures easily but is less precarious to use as an arch stone than as a lintel.

The door to the right of the church, at no. 4, is occasionally open, usually an hour before 6:00 P.M. mass.

This is the entrance to the plant-filled thirteenth-century cloister. Along the walls is a display of Gothic doorframe pieces and a nineteenth-century marble tomb marker.

If you are facing the façade of the church, turn right down via San Remigio. At the end of this lane is the wider and busier street, via de' Neri. At this intersection you have several possibilities for eating—all depending on your pocketbook and taste. (If you aren't hungry at this juncture, skip to page 104.) If you are interested in a more than moderately priced restaurant, turn right for a short detour to Il Fagiano ("The Pheasant") at via de' Neri 57/r. This street is also crowded with *alimentari*, small neighborhood grocery stores. Just around the left corner from via San Remigio, at no. 44/r, is a *salumeria*, another name for "grocery store." We're approaching the end of the second walk, and a take-out meal could be enjoyed on the Ponte alle Grazie, which overlooks the Arno River. Pick out some prosciutto, cheeses, and ask for a few *panini* (small sandwiches). Buy a bottle of red or white wine, and you have the makings of a classic picnic. Another store with a slightly wider selection of meats and cheeses is at no. 35/r; it's a *pizzicheria*. Literally translated it means a "cheesemonger's shop." If you're more inclined to sit at tables and chairs, start walking down via de' Neri until you reach no. 17/r on the left side of the street. Your destination will be a usually lively, updated *fiaschetteria*, or "wine restaurant."

As you're walking you may want to consider how the street came to be called via de' Neri. Condemned prisoners in the Middle Ages were marched from their cells in the Bargello down through this street, across Borgo Santa Croce, and out past the city walls for execution. A sympathetic band of companions formed to accompany the prisoners on their last walk through Florence. They called themselves the *Compagnia dei Neri* ("The Companions in Black"), and the street took on their name.

If you eat lunch or dinner at the *fiaschetteria* Niccolini, you'll order (or point at, depending on your Italian vocabulary) the buffet dishes displayed on the front counter. Their summer specialty is cold rice with artichoke hearts, diced ham, and fresh vegetables. A carafe of wine and American-style cheesecake are in order here. Depending on how friendly you feel when you come in, you may want to sit at a large table and share it with others. Most of the Italians (and numerous other foreign diners) who come in here are young, well traveled, and keen on trying out their English and discussing American movies or New York City.

An older, portly woman, who could easily pass as the prototypical concierge if she were in Paris, sits, or more often sleeps, at a corner table in the back. Her pug dog also sleeps near her table. The restaurant always feels empty when she has not yet arrived for her daily *fiasco di vino*.

Twenty-five yards down the road from the *fiaschetteria* is the intersection of via de' Neri and via dei Benci. Look toward your left and across the street at the corner of via dei Benci and Borgo Santa Croce and you'll see a tower and loggia, or open porch. The Alberti family reigned over this fourteenth-century working-class neighborhood. The tower was once one of their chief residences and the loggia that you see is a fifteenth-century reconstruction of their thirteenth-century porch. When the Alberti sided with the striking woolworkers during the bloody "Ciompi" riots of 1378, their loggia was destroyed, and they were deported from Florence for their liberal ties with the low-paid working class. Cosimo de' Medici kindly invited them back to Florence in 1434 mostly because their wealth and popularity were sorely missed.

The most illustrious of the family was the fifteenth-century architect Leon Battista Alberti. His designs for the façade of the Church of Santa Maria Novella and the Palazzo Rucellai, the first Renaissance-style palace, have kept his name in art history annals for centuries. Alberti also wrote one of the first known treatises on architecture. His house is at the very end of this walk and can be seen from the Ponte alle Grazie.

The Alberti loggia is now a café, and has been for well over a hundred years. Back in the fifteenth century, the same space was rented out to the Michelangelo of blacksmiths in Florence: Grosso Niccolo, better remembered as "*il Caparra*," "the Earnest One." His iron lanterns adorn the outsides of the most opulent palaces in town. The Strozzi Palace, in the center of Florence, and the Guadagni Palace are the two most

Fifteenth-century Alberti loggia-turned-café (corner of via dei Benci and Borgo Santa Croce)

famous structures that have his work still on view. "Il Caparra" acquired his nickname not because he himself was known for his honesty, but because his wealthy customers were in the habit of ordering elaborate ornaments and then neglecting to pay. The canny artisan made it his business practice to pick up the total bill for his handicraft before the work was finished; he took on the name of "the Earnest One" as a way of explaining this practice. Many of the iron rings, flag and torch holders, and hitching posts that you see on Florentine palaces were also wrought in his workshop.

The café at the Alberti loggia is worth a stop if for nothing more than a look at the clientele. There's a dark back room with boisterous pool-playing always in progress. The waiters and waitresses sport a quizzical "anything-can-happen-in-this-place" demeanor. The jukebox music is loud, and the coffee is strong.

Continue strolling down via dei Benci in the direction of the Arno. The first cross street on your left, directly oppostie via de' Neri, is Corso de' Tintori, the old dye-works district for the Renaissance silk and wool industry. The street's name translates into "Course of the Dyers." The *corso* eventually runs into a piazza where the dyeing materials from the shops would drain into the Arno. Twenty yards from via dei Benci, at Corso de' Tintori 47/r, is the restaurant Fagioli. The food is good and moderately priced, but there's a minimum charge of L12,000.

The fifteenth-century palace on the corner of Corso de' Tintori at via dei Benci 6 was once owned by the Alberti clan and is now the Museo Horne ("The Horne Museum"). A sprawling newspaper stand is usually set up in front of the palace. The architect of the Museo Horne was probably "Cronaca" (Simone dell Pollaiolo), who also designed the Strozzi Palace. The hours of the museum are irregular: Mondays and Thursdays from 10:00 A.M. to 1:00 P.M. and 3:00 P.M. to 5:00 P.M.

Herbert Percy Horne, the last private owner of the palace, was an early-twentieth-century English art critic, collector, and friend to the legendary art connoisseur Bernard Berenson. In old age the two quarreled over the attribution of four fifteenth-century altarpiece panels. The works in question had been retrieved from a fourteenth-century Florentine convent founded by retired prostitutes and are now owned by the Philadelphia Museum of Art. Horne adamantly believed that the panels were by fifteenth-century artist Sandro Botticelli, and he advised the well-to-do American collector, John G. Johnson, to purchase the paintings. Soon after this negotiation had taken place, Berenson announced to the art world that the panels had actually been executed by the obscure artist, "Amico di Sandro," presumably a friend and coworker of Botticelli.

Years of silence followed between the two scholars. Then, one day Berenson happened to have taken a trip to London and while strolling through the National Gallery he spotted two early paintings by Botticelli. The resemblance between the pieces in front of him and the four disputed panels now in the United States was undeniable. Berenson there and then decided to publish a retraction of his earlier statement on the altarpiece paintings. When he returned to Florence, however, he heard word of Horne's imminent death. Berenson learned that Horne had been moved to the nearby villa of a friend, and in an uncharacteristic gesture of reconciliation he appeared uninvited at the door to see his old colleague. Berenson and Horne talked, shook hands, and later that night, after the visitor had left, Horne died. The palace and most of the art collection were left to the city of Florence. The rooms are studded with Sienese masters and a sampling of Della Robbias, Daddi, Lorenzetti, and an altar *predella*, or "platform," painted by Masolino and Masaccio.

Across the street from the Museo Horne, on via dei Benci, are two more grandiose Alberti houses that extend all the way down the 100 yards or so to the river and the Ponte alle Grazie.

The best time of day to wander out on the bridge is at early sunset. Florentines, finished with their daily activities, stroll down to the bridge and fish in the shallow waters or row along the quays in trim, canoelike boats. Under the right side of the bridge you'll see a cement barrier extending the span of the river. This is called a *pescaia*, a place where the greatest number of fish congregate. River water that flows over the cement barrier turns into mild rapids. A large amount of oxygen is trapped inside these rapids and fish head for it. Serious fishermen, decked out in rubber hip-high boots, wade out across the *pescaia* and wait for the fish to jump onto their lines.

In medieval days, barges of lumber would flow down the Arno from the forest hills around Florence and stop at the far end of the bridge where a sawmill and woodworkers' studio were located.

The first bridge on this spot was built in 1235. The mayor of Florence at that time was named Rubaconte da Mandella, and the structure was christened the Ponte Rubaconte. The thirteenth-century bridge had nine arches supporting it. On the via dei Benci side of the bridge was a small chapel built by the Alberti family in 1372. Displayed in it was a much-loved tabernacle with a painting of the Madonna and Child. The bridge then became known as Ponte alle Grazie, or "The Bridge of the Graces," in honor of the Madonna's visage watching over the passageway.

Seven tiny chapels were also built along both sides of the bridge in the fourteenth century. They were inhabited by nuns who were disgusted with life in the Florentine convents. Morals among the ecclesiastical brothers and sisters were loose if not completely unhinged. The small band of nuns moved out onto the bridge; food was passed to them through the barred windows of the chapels they lived in. Gradually more and more nuns joined them and their order. "The Romite" ("Female Hermits"), became so enlarged that they had to move off the bridge and into a convent around the corner from the Church of Santa Croce. Artisans and merchants took over the abandoned chapels for the next few centuries. On August 4, 1944, the Germans bombed the thirteenth-century bridge to pieces. The bridge that we're standing on now is a reproduction of the original structure, minus the lady hermits' chapels.

Leon Battista Alberti's sixteenth-century palace is the corner building to the left of via dei Benci.

Look to your left from the Ponte alle Grazie and up toward the hill. You'll see the twelfth-century marble-and-gold-faced Church of San Miniato. The Italian Romanesque church was named for an early Christian martyr who was fed to the lions in the old amphitheater.

Dante often strolled along the thirteenth-century bridge that spanned the Arno on this spot. He lived in an era when Florence was rocking with political scandals and corruption. From the vantage point of the bridge, Dante gazed up at San Miniato, "the church . . . above the Rubaconte" (as he wrote in *The Divine Comedy*), and he pondered the ill fate of such a materialistic society.

Two hundred years later, another citizen whose name is synonymous with Florence—Michelangelo— was busy piling mattresses and bales of wool around the sixteenth-century bell tower next to the church. Florence was under attack from the Spanish troops of Charles V, and the Renaissance artist, along with a small band of maverick soldiers, was defending the highest point of the besieged city and protecting an architectural treasure against gunfire. Two long-necked cannons were hauled up to the belfry windows, and Michelangelo and his men proceeded to blast away at the advancing Spanish soldiers for several days. One enemy gunman, however, was successful in hitting and setting fire to the mattresses and layers of wool padding. Within minutes the bell tower high above the city streets was a beacon of flames. The Spanish soldiers drew back in horror at the blaze burning so brilliantly next to the ancient martyr's church. Michelangelo and his men scrambled down from the smoking tower and flew to the safety of another belfry in the Church of San Niccolò at the bottom of the hillside.

Despite this valiant gesture on the part of the artist and his compatriots, the Spaniards gained control of Florence and the foreigners continued to rule the city for well over a century. Our walk ends on this bridge but if you find yourself wandering up through the hillsides to San Miniato be sure to walk over to the bell tower and examine the still charred walls of Michelangelo's last stand.

Walk

3

Markets,
Bazaars,
and Antiques

○

Starting Point: Corner of via Nazionale and via dell'Ariento

The third walk begins 400 yards to the right of the Florence train station on the corner of via Nazionale and via dell'Ariento.

Posted above the fountain and overlooking the entrance to Florence's sprawling market area is a rainbow-hued terra-cotta tabernacle encrusted with flowers, fruits, cherubs, saints, heads popping out of the ceramic frame, and, smack in the center, an unruffled Madonna and her sweet-faced Child. This street shrine is known as "The Tabernacle of Fonticine" ("*Tabernacolo delle Fonticine*"). It was placed here in 1522 by a social, semireligious group known as the "Men of the Kingdom of Bethlehem." The artist was Giovanni della Robbia, the last of the three generations of the famous ceramic sculpturing family in Florence. Not only was he the last, but, in art history circles, he's considered the least. Adjectives such as *theatrical, decadent, gaudy, mawkish*, and *unbalanced* are often used in stylistic analyses of his work. Giovanni's forte was business, not art.

His grandfather, Luca, born in 1399 or 1400, was the founder of the della Robbia dynasty and studios. Apprenticed to Lorenzo Ghiberti (creator of the famed Bronze Doors of the Baptistery), Luca readily learned goldsmithing at an early age. He later spent ten years working on the interior decoration of the Duomo.

The art of glazing terra-cotta is an ancient one, and Luca was an innovator in applying the technique to sculpture and sculptural ornaments for Florentine churches and hospitals.

In 1446 Luca and his brother Marco and their brood of wives, children, servants, and apprentices moved into a block of houses about 100 yards to the right of the tabernacle on via Guelfa. For several centuries this stretch of the street was formally known as via della Robbia. When Marco died at a young age and left the support of his family to Luca, the fatherless nephews and nieces were put to work in the ceramic studios.

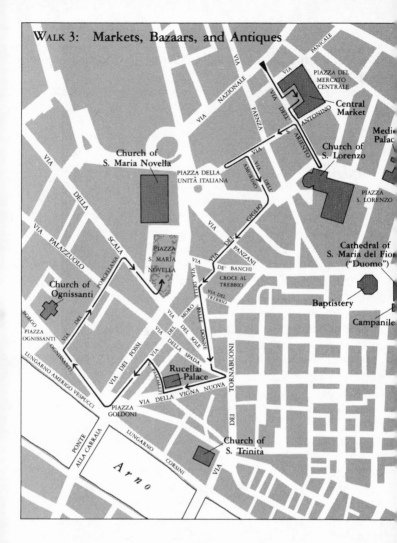

Andrea, Marco's eldest son, showed artistic talent, and Luca made him a full-fledged apprentice and then partner.

Luca was the true Italian patriarch. He ruled tyrannously over his home and workshops while designing elegant, austere, Greek-classical-looking sculptures until his death at eighty-three.

Andrea was quieter and less demanding of himself and others. His terra-cotta reliefs are soft, sensual, and serene; his business sense was equally relaxed. Andrea did produce seven sons, and all were recruited into the family business. Only Giovanni managed to have any interest in the *bottega*, and then his enthusiasm was mostly oriented toward the profits rather than the

aesthetics. Two of Andrea's sons ran off to join the Dominican friars, and they quietly puttered away at their
pottery within the hushed walls of the Convent of San
Marco.

Between business deals and investments Giovanni
did manage to chisel away at a few pieces, and this
tabernacle is probably the best known if not the best
regarded of all his work. (One tabernacle is in the
Church of SS. Apostoli, and another is plastered on the
front of a palace in the Borgo San Jacopo.)

Maud Cruttwell, a turn-of-the-century British della
Robbia scholar, disdainfully dismisses this tabernacle
as an artless disaster:

> We have on the same plane figures in no less than five
> different scales of proportion. Rigid and trivial, they stand
> out like wax dolls, and the very realism of their colouring,
> instead of animating them, adds to their artificial lifeless
> appearance. It would be difficult to condemn sufficiently
> the inartistic design of the frame with the huge prominent
> heads projecting from disjointed scraps of garlands which
> crush their weight down upon the tiny statuettes below.

Continue down the via dell'Ariento and you'll get
your first whiff of daily market life in Florence.

Down a block on your left is the block-long, glass-
roof Mercato Centrale ("Central Market"). The best
time to plunge into this indoor food coliseum is early
morning (and the earlier the better).

The latter half of the nineteenth century was the era
of colossal urban building. London's Crystal Palace, in
1851, cleared the way for grandiose galleries of glass.
Milan's enclosed marketplace, the Galleria, was the
height of shopping elegance in nineteenth-century Italy and the envy of style-conscious Florentines.

The Old Market of Florence became, over the centuries, an eyesore and a major health hazard. When an
epidemic of cholera broke out in 1835, plans were has-
tened to tear down the shops and stalls and relocate
the market outside the center of Florence. The architect of Milan's Galleria, Giuseppe Mengoni, was commissioned to design the ultimate in cosmopolitan
marketplaces: a spacious indoor pavilion topped by a
glass-paned skylight roof. The building was completed
in 1874 and displayed to the world as Florence's statement on tasteful food shopping. But then an embarrassing situation developed. Not a single pork vendor

or vegetable salesman wanted to move from the Old Market and set up quarters in the newfangled market. They liked the Old Market just fine. For the next eleven years, after the grand opening of the Central Market, the luxurious indoor shopping mall remained vacant with the exception of an occasional flower show.

By 1885, however, the Florentine city fathers could no longer stand the profitless public structure. Orders for the Old Market to be torn down were put into effect. Architectural plans were drawn for high-class, high-rent stores to replace the ramshackle shops and stalls of the Old Market. The butchers and produce merchants had no choice but to relocate in the Central Market. Many of the businesses inside the market today are the third generation of the first group of merchants who reluctantly settled into the indoor comforts of the Central Market.

Walk inside and wind your way around the marble-countered poultry, fish, and meat stands. You'll see some of the original nineteenth-century booths with gold-lettered signs, brass scales, and hanging glass lamps.

Walk or take the escalator up to the second floor; it was added to the building when the Central Market began to catch on with Florentine merchants. Stroll around the aisles of artichokes, eggplants, plum tomatoes, zucchinis, and bouquets of parsley, rosemary, basil, and fennel. Apricots, oranges, peaches, melons, and figs are piled in pyramids or tucked into frilly paper cups. Fresh sprigs of leaves are draped around the meticulous rows of vegetables and fruits to make every display look like a sunny patch of Tuscan garden. Look closely at the cardboard, handmade signs propped up in the mounds of produce. When a merchant has written *"Nostrali"* ("Ours") he means to tell you that the beans or tomatoes come directly from his own farm. More emphatic produce vendors write *"Veri nostrali"* ("Truly ours"). If there is even the slightest doubt cast about the provenance of the vegetables, the farmer will write *"Nostrali lo* giuro!" ("These are ours, I *swear* it!").

A small café with tables and chairs is in an alcove to the side of the large floor. Nineteenth-century photographs of the Central Market hang along the walls.

Inside the Mercato Centrale (via dell'Ariento)

Exit from the main entrance of the Central Market on via dell'Ariento, turn left, and walk about 30 yards toward via S. Antonino.

Wrapped around the Central Market and along via dell'Ariento is an Arab bazaar of cotton shirts, leather bags and belts, Indian gauze dresses, and assorted plastic kitchenware, glasses, and straw baskets.

Contine walking about 75 yards down via dell'Ariento to Piazza San Lorenzo, an open square in front of the Church of San Lorenzo and the Medici Tombs. Have a seat on the low wall next to the church directly under the bell tower of the basilica, and read a few pages ahead for a brief history of the Medicis and their role in the art life of Florence.

Brunelleschi's fifteenth-century Church of San Lorenzo stands on the site of what was one of the oldest religious structures in Florence: a fourth-century Christian basilica that was built outside the shadow of the old city wall. In the eleventh century the basilica was rebuilt and enlarged. By the fifteenth century, Florentines were eager to construct something even more impressive in this neighborhood.

Rows of working-class houses were demolished to make room for the larger foundation of this new

Used clothing stall outside the Mercato Centrale

church. Giovanni de' Medici, the richest man on the block, chipped in the money for the sacristy. The date 1418 marks the beginning of the construction of San Lorenzo and the first time that the Medicis parted with money to act as patrons of the arts.

Giovanni's son, Cosimo, inherited a bundle from his father, and proceeded to increase his savings account by lending out vast sums of money at high interest rates. In the eyes of the Renaissance church, however, usury was a serious sin. Cosimo was guilt-ridden and nervous about his money-making activities, and he tried to alleviate these feelings by not hounding his debtors too often for swift repayment. He once penned a note to his "Maker": "Only have patience with me, my Lord, and I shall return it all to you." A man of his word, Cosimo began pouring thousands of gold florins into the decoration of San Lorenzo, and then he was crushed to hear that more money had been spent on older medieval churches several centuries before his generosity. This Medici patron was a familiar, friendly figure to the community of artists working around Florence in the mid-fifteenth century; he kept a close eye on various projects going on in town. Cosimo was excited by the two biggest enterprises in the art world: Brunelleschi began building the red-domed cupola for the cathedral in 1420, and Ghiberti was casting the Bronze Doors of the Baptistery in 1425. Michelozzo Michelozzi was commissioned by Cosimo to enlarge the Church and Convent of San Marco in 1437, and Fra Angelico was asked to paint frescoes on the walls of the monastery over the next decade. Cosimo's great friend was the sculptor Donatello. When the Medici ruler heard that the Florentine artist was temporarily out of work, he immediately hired Donatello to design and create two massive bronze pulpits, eight glazed terra-cotta wall plaques, and a set of intricately cast bronze doors, all for the Basilica of San Lorenzo.

Piero ("The Gouty") de' Medici did not share his father's passion for charity, building, or artistic friends. He spent his days making himself unpopular by trying to collect all the overdue loans that Cosimo had so nobly overlooked. Piero did commission a piece of artwork that is today one of the favorite masterpieces in all of Florence: *The Journey of the Magi* in the Medici Chapel of the family palace on via Cavour. Records show, however, that the artist, Benozzo Gozzoli, had trouble getting advance money out of the tightfisted Piero. The work came to a standstill at one point because Benozzo ran out of gold and ultramarine paint. Piero also was very fussy. One letter from the painter to the patron, dated 1459, shows the extent to which Piero ruled over the artistic endeavor:

> Yesterday I had a letter from your Magnificence . . . from which I understand that you think that the serafims I made are out of place. I have only made one in a corner among certain clouds; one sees nothing but the tip of his wings, and he is so well hidden and so covered by clouds that he does not make for deformity at all but rather for beauty. . . . I have made another on the other side of the altar but also hidden in a similar way. Ruberto Martegli has seen them and said that there is no reason to make a fuss about them. Nevertheless, I'll do as you command; two little cloudlets will take them away . . .

Piero's son, Lorenzo de' Medici, had made friends with various members of the Florentine art world. He counted among his faithful court members Verrocchio, who repaired the palace antiques for him, Botticelli, and the young Michelangelo. Lorenzo treated the aging and virtually unrecognized sculptor Bertoldo as a respected uncle and invited him to travel and live amidst the Medici family circle. On the other hand, Lorenzo completely ignored the presence of Leonardo da Vinci in Florence, and the future genius of the Renaissance era was forced to move to Milan for social acceptance and active patronage.

The Medici family continued to build and embellish Florence well into the eighteenth century. In 1740, Anna Maria Ludovica, officially referred to as "The Electress Palatine" and historically remembered as "The Last Medici," ordered the construction of the bell tower for the Church of San Lorenzo.

Anna Maria was the very model of an art patroness despite a gloomy and virtually uneventful life. Married off to a German prince at a tender age, Anna Maria soon discovered that even her honeymoon was no bargain; she was bedridden for weeks after the wedding ceremony with a malady attributed to a "poison he [the prince] had imbibed from Venus's shell." The marriage was childless, and the prince died in early middle age. Anna Maria's mission in life was to supervise the building of the *campanile* and the interior decoration of the Medici mausoleum inside the basilica.

The Electress Palatine spent her last quiet years ensconced in a suite of Baroque-encrusted, marble-floored rooms in the depths of the Pitti Palace. Propped up on velvet pillows under the flowing draperies of a black canopy tent, she received visiting royalty and a few family friends. She died in 1743. Horace Mann was residing in Florence at the time, and he wrote in his daily journal: ". . . The Electress died about an hour ago . . . the poor remains of the Medici is [*sic*] soon to join her ancestors . . ."

The Medici dynasty's loss was unquestionably Florence's gain: Anna Maria's will left every Medici art treasure to the city of Florence. Her last testament was specific: not one statue or canvas was ever to leave Florence. The Medici collection "should be for the benefit of the public of all nations." The Uffizi Gallery and the museums of the Pitti Palace and the Bargello are amply decorated with the objects of Anna Maria's last thoughtful gesture.

Stroll back along via dell'Ariento for the continuation of our walk. This street was, until the fifteenth century, the medieval quarter of the silversmiths. Once narrow and dark, and nothing more than an alleyway, via dell'Ariento was widened only in the late nineteenth century for better access to the Central Market.

Turn left down via S. Antonino for more marketing sights and smells. Food and wine stores line both sides of this stone-paved street and shoppers zigzag from one storefront to another loading straw baskets with paper-wrapped cheese and meats.

The first cross street along via S. Antonino is via Faenza. Look to your left and you'll see at the corner a large tabernacle and a marble plaque next to it with the inscription: *"Elemosine per il Mantenimento della Luce"* ("Alms for the maintenance of the lights"). This is where the devout could contribute a few lire to keep the oil lamps burning in the evening hours.

The second street to your left on via S. Antonino is via dell'Amorino, or the "Street of the Sweetheart." The romantic name for this byway was chosen because a favored but unidentifiable mistress of Florence's sixteenth-century political commentator, Niccolò Machiavelli, once lived here. Before exploring this tiny street and the historical details of Machiavelli's behavior outside the political arena, walk a few more yards down via S. Antonino (and then return later to this intersection).

At no. 11, on your right, is a palazzo with stone scrolls unfurled against the first two stories of the house. Known as the Palazzo dei Cartelloni ("Palace of the Placards"), the building was once the house of Galileo's protégé and first biographer, Vincenzo Viviani. As a young boy in the early seventeenth century, Viviani lived with Galileo's family. His education was rigorously supervised by the astronomer, and Viviani always referred to himself as "Galileo's last disciple." Viviani's great contribution to science was a mathematical treatise entitled *De maximis et minimis* (*Of things large and small*), which was published in Florence in 1659. The opus with this intriguing title is actually a detailed account of the intricacies of conic sections—circles, ellipses, parabolas, and hyperbolas.

Galileo's bust looks over the front entrance of the palace. One of the placards praises Galileo's scientific contributions; the other acknowledges the graciousness of Louis XIV of France, who provided Viviani with a handsome pension until the scientist's death at the age of eighty.

Head back in the other direction. A few yards away is a small rococo chapel on the right side of the street. There's no street number for the chapel, but the front door is directly opposite Hotel City. The door to the Oratorio di S. Giuseppe ("Chapel of St. Joseph") is generally open during morning market hours but may be closed all afternoon. A number of saints are honored within this tiny space but the female shoppers who stop inside on their daily rounds are usually lighting a candle for Saint Anthony, the patron saint of marriage. Young boys and girls are often the only attendants in this eighteenth-century chapel. If you drop in for a moment, it's courteous to leave 100 lire as a donation.

Continue walking to via dell'Amorino, the scene of some of Machiavelli's amatory adventures. Early in the shopping day you'll see the stalls of the fabric merchants and clusters of women knee-deep in fabrics all around the tables.

Much of what we know about Machiavelli's private life comes from his correspondence with his closest comrade, Francesco Vettori. Machiavelli shunned the business life of Florence for a career in foreign affairs and political journalism. His diplomatic wanderings took him to the courts of France and the Papal City, and he was a military adviser for Florence's final conquest of Pisa in 1509. Machiavelli's criticisms of Medici governmental manipulations earned him a jail term and finally early retirement to a country farm beyond the hills of Florence.

In 1513, while basking in bucolic bliss, the political writer composed his classic series of essays, *The Prince*, in which he advocated a unified state and strong, compassionate leadership. During his political exile Machiavelli managed to make frequent clandestine trips into Florence. His two favorite companions in town were a Florentine shopkeeper, Donato del Corno, and a longtime mistress, "La Riccia," "the Curly-haired One," who may have been the "sweetheart" referred to in the name of this street. The letters exchanged between Machiavelli and Vettori touched on many subjects; their love affairs were always the

most heated topics of discussion. When Vettori w......
of his hesitation in following up on a newly formed li-
aison with a young Florentine belle, Machiavelli enthusiastically urged him on:

> . . . I beg you: follow your star . . . for I believe, used to
> believe and always will believe that what Boccaccio says
> is true: that it is better to act and repent, than do nothing
> and repent.

Continue down via dell'Amorino but stop at the
end of the street. The next few streets on our walk will
follow a zigzag course. Double-check the street signs
and my directions as you negotiate the turns.

At the end of via dell'Amorino is the cross street
via del Melarancio. A *melarancio* is a pomegranate,
and the name refers to a medieval orchard that was
once along this route. Walk past this street and also
past a large arched wooden door to the palazzo on
your right. Turn right onto via del Giglio, "Street of
the Lily."

Forty yards down via del Giglio on the right side of
the street is the Palazzo Gaddi. The street number is
13, and the palace is directly opposite the side street
via dell'Alloro. Renaissance Florentines nicknamed
this residence the "Paradiso Gaddi" because of its
sumptuous furnishings and sybaritic social gatherings.
A small plaque on the outside wall says that John Milton, the seventeenth-century English poet and author
of *Paradise Lost*, once lived here. The historical anno-
tation is probably a slight embellishment. Milton was
known to have passed many hours in the palace at the
famous meetings of a literary academy, but whether or
not he actually resided in the palace is still open to
question.

Milton set out for his tour of the continent in the
spring of 1638 funded by his father, who had requested a decent collection of original Italian musical
scores. Florence was the young poet's mecca. He believed it to be a secluded spot on Italian soil where
educated citizens continued to pursue the very best in
thought, beauty, and conversation. Milton was far
from disappointed with the Florentine intellectual cli-
mate, but the religious intolerance disturbed him. A
century and a half before his arrival, a Florentine Dominican friar, Girolamo Savonarola, accused the papa-

cy of licentiousness; he was burned at the stake in Piazza della Signoria. In 1517 Martin Luther nailed his ninety-five theses to the door of the Wittenberg Church in Germany and northern Europe splintered from the Roman papal rule. The Catholic Church was faced with a rebellion, and the only solution was to tighten control over the remaining flock.

Throughout the seventeenth century Roman Catholic tribunals, more popularly known as "The Inquisition," made it their business to discourage disagreement with Church philosophies and Church authority. The study and practice of science—science that went against Church principles—was unacceptable. This is where Galileo and other seventeenth-century pursuers of scientific theory ran up against the Church bureaucracy. Galileo was a hearty supporter of Copernicus and his revolutionary theory that the earth revolves around the sun. In 1633, the astronomer was called before the Roman Inquisition. The Church officials accused him of advocating the research of Copernicus over the words of the Bible. Threatened with torture at the age of seventy, Galileo decided to renounce his scientific beliefs, superficially at least. At the end of his trial he was forced to kneel in front of his inquisitors and declare that the earth remained in one spot and was the center of the universe. As he slowly rose to his feet, however, he turned to a companion standing next to him and muttered: *"Eppur si muove!"* ("But it *does* move!"). Under house arrest for the last eight years of his life, Galileo retired quietly to Arcetri, a small town outside Florence. He was permitted to stay in his Florentine townhouse on Costa San Giorgio (next to the Belvedere Fortress) only when his failing eyesight required medical attention.

Unsympathetic with the Church's tyrannous measures against the advancement of science, Milton's first social call in Florence was on the aging and nearly blind Galileo. The Florentine intelligentsia was far more tolerant of the scientific marvels that were being introduced in the Renaissance. Cultural societies, or "academies," were springing up around the city in the seventeenth century and the members met in each others' palaces to discuss poetry, politics, and paintings. Galileo was well received within these academies, and he was often asked to read papers on his multifarious inventions: the laws of weights, the pendulum, the proportional compass, and the telescope.

The Palazzo Gaddi was the setting for the academy of the "Svolgliati" ("The Disgusted"). Jacopo Gaddi, the host of the palace and founder of "The Disgusted," was exemplary in both roles. John Arthos, in his scholarly work *Milton and the Italian Cities*, writes:

> Jacopo Gaddi seems to have been the intellectual and social arbiter of the city, second in importance only to the Grand Duke himself.

Costly antiques, rare books, and canvases by Leonardo da Vinci and del Sarto filled the Gaddi salons. Exotic floral and sculptural gardens stretched out behind the palazzo into what is now via del Melarancio. European plants of every variety and strange specimens from along the banks of Egypt's Nile River bloomed behind Gaddi's Palace.

It was within the confines of this palace of luxury and learning that Milton dazzled Florentine society with his linguistic and poetic prowess. He knew Italian impeccably, as well as Spanish, French, Latin, and Greek. In September of 1638, Milton enthralled the members of "The Disgusted" with his verses in Latin hexameters. The poem was acclaimed as "*molto eru-*

"Wine" or "beggars'" windows (via del Giglio 2)

dita" and Florence's foremost poet at the time, Antonio Malatesta, presented Milton with a collection of his works, *La Tina* ("fifty somewhat obscene sonnets").

Cross the same street, keep walking, and look for no. 2. To the left of the front door and under the window is a small wooden trapdoor. Bottles of wine were sold and passed through this small opening by the merchant or owner of the palace who operated a *cantina* or "wine cellar" below the street level. These tiny doors are also called "beggars' windows." At night it was customary for the wealthy merchant to leave a few bits of food and maybe a half-consumed bottle of wine for the poorer folk. You'll see wine windows or beggars' windows all over Florence, but some of these architectural features have been recycled for use as mailboxes or enclosures for apartment doorbells. This one on via del Giglio is unusual for its clever design. The wine window is surrounded by a miniature stone palazzo, and the small opening appears to be the great arched doorway of the mansion. Above the miniature palazzo is the merchant's sign: *"Vendita di Vino"* ("Sale of Wine").

A few feet down from the wine window is a medieval passageway called chiasso degli Armati. The shadowy stone archways, smoky-glass windows, and rambling rooms that bridge over and into buildings next door make this alleyway look like a setting from a North African *Casbah*.

Walk to the intersection of via del Giglio and via Panzani, and cross the street. On the left side of the block is one of Florence's most renowned department stores, Standa. It's a rare place in town where a customer can buy almost anything under one roof, and this convenience is still a great novelty to Florentines.

Follow via del Giglio for a few more yards, but stop at the next intersection with via de' Banchi.

The palace around the left corner of this junction, at no. 4, is our next stop. This was the sixteenth-century home of the Marquis of Mondragone, the Spanish tutor of Francesco, son of Cosimo I, and a royal cupid of sorts. The palace is a romantic landmark in Florentine history as it was the first lovers' tryst for Francesco and his fiery Venetian seductress Bianca Cappello.

Bianca's life story is a Cinderella-like tale. Born to a wealthy and noble family in Venice, she grew up, as

Chiasso degli Armati

the age-old story goes, to become a dark-eyed, bewitching beauty. Across from the family's Venetian palace was the neighborhood bank; the young maiden's curious eye was caught by the comings and goings of a humble bank clerk named Bonaventura. With the assistance of her maid, Bianca managed to make the acquaintance of the clerk, and soon after she was slipping over to his room every night. One evening she crept back to the palace only to discover the great wooden door closed and bolted for the night. Bianca ran back to Bonaventura's room, explained the embarrassing situation to him, and convinced him to run off to Florence with her.

Once in Florence the couple settled in with some of the bank clerk's relatives who lived near Piazza San Marco. Bianca's life then took a turn for the worse. Her role in the Bonaventura household was little more than that of a housemaid. She scrubbed and swept her days away probably wishing that she had never seen or heard of a bank clerk. Then, when spring arrived in

Florence, she developed the habit of relaxing outside the house and gazing at the pedestrians, most of whom were on their way to the Church of San Marco. And who should be among the daily throng but Francesco de' Medici, the heir apparent to the Grand Duchy of Tuscany. He spotted the lovely Bianca and immediately began to plot a way to meet her under more acceptable social circumstances. The young Medici hit on the idea of asking his tutor, Mondragone, to arrange a rendezvous at this palace, and here the couple were formally introduced.

The friendship developed, and Francesco was so charmed by Bianca's company that he bought her a glorious palace of her own on via Maggio. He even went so far as to find a nice secretarial job at his court for Bonaventura. Some months after this cozy arrangement was made, Francesco's wife Giovanna died. It was only a matter of time before Bonaventura met his untimely end. He was found murdered in a street behind Bianca's palace.

There was a short court mourning, and then Francesco and Bianca were married in the Duomo amidst pomp and splendor. Bianca was crowned the Grand Duchess of Tuscany, and her hometown, Venice, forgave her earlier indiscretions and named her a Daughter of the Republic of Venice and San Marco. When a princely son, Antonio, was born to the couple, however, Medici family intrigue intervened. Francesco's brother, Cardinal Ferdinando, was already displeased at not being elected pope and, in an impious gesture, poisoned both Francesco and Bianca during a dinner party at their country villa. The cardinal took over the reins of the Florentine government, buried Bianca in a lowly grave, and relieved little Antonio of his family responsibilities to the throne.

This streetcorner is known even today as Canto del Mondragone, the "Mondragone Corner," in honor of the Spanish matchmaker.

Don't turn down via de' Banchi. Our walk resumes along the curving via del Moro, which is across from via del Giglio. Look for a collection of motorcycles parked on the left side of via del Moro, and you'll know that you're headed in the right direction.

The short trek through via del Moro ends in one of the tiniest squares in Florence, the Croce al Trebbio

("Cross at the Three Streets"). You can't miss the granite column planted in the center of the intersection. Acanthus leaves embellish the lower part of the column, and perched on top is a white marble cross etched with bas-reliefs. The column and cross were set up on this spot in 1308 to honor St. Peter Martyr, who routed a group of heretics, the "Paterini," from Florence in the thirteenth century.

If you're facing the column with a glimpse of the Church of Santa Maria Novella on your right, walk to the left of the monument and down one of Florence's most melodically-named streets, via delle Belle Donne, the "Street of the Beautiful Women." Check the street sign here, as there are several turnoffs at this intersection. For further identification, look for the palace on the right of the entrance to this street that has the bookstore Franco Maria Ricci on its ground floor.

Before strolling down via delle Belle Donne, face the palace on the left entrance to the street. Look above you, on the palace wall, and you'll spot an open-mouthed gargoyle. His mate is farther down the street on the opposite side of the house. Below the gargoyle and on the left wall of the palace is a shoulder-height marble plaque to show you how high the 1966 flood rose in this square. Continue looking along the wall and you'll see the very distinct line left by the muddy floodwaters.

It's generally assumed that the street earned its enchanting name from a particularly renowned Renaissance brothel once located on this block. There's also a nineteenth-century narrative about the neighborhood that is predictably puritanical and rosy in its interpretation:

> In the via delle Belle Donne there was a very large old house in which were many lodgers male and female . . . Among these were many very pretty girls, some of them seamstresses, others corset-makers, some milliners, all employed in shops, who worked all day and then went out in the evening to carry their sewing to the "magazzini." And it was from them that the street got its name, for it became so much the fashion to go and look at them that young men would say, "Andiamo nelle via delle Belle Donne"—"Let's go to the Street of the Beautiful Women"; so it has been so-called to this day.
>
> And when they sallied forth they were at once sur-

rounded or joined by young men who sought their company with views more or less honorable, as is usual.

As you're sallying forth down via delle Belle Donne, look on your left a ways down for a palace doorway marked no. 8. Next to the entrance is a doorbell framed in a marble plaque that's engraved with the words "*Campanello della Scuderia*" ("Small bell to the stables"). This was the stable-door entrance to this grand palace; the bell was used to ring for a horse-drawn carriage and liveried groom. In the summer months the door is usually wide open, revealing what is now an ordinary garage for cars and motorcycles. Be sure to take note of the meticulously painted black-and-white geometric patterns covering the walls and ceiling of the entranceway to these once-elegant stables.

Next door to the frescoed garage is a small family-run restaurant and *fiaschetteria* (wine café) called Mescita di Vini.

Go down the left side of via delle Belle Donne all the way to the end. Just before turning the corner to your left onto via della Spada, look on the palace wall to your left. Another more conventional-looking wine window is set into the wall here. A marble-inlaid sign above the little wooden door gives the hours that the *cantina* is open during the summer and winter months. Across the street from the wine window, at no. 5/r, is the American Express Bank.

Continue, to the left, down the 25 yards of via della Spada. You'll end up at the very busy intersection of via dei Tornabuoni; the back wall of the Palazzo Strozzi is in front of you to your right.

Our right-hand turnoff is via della Vigna Nuova. The massive palace in which American Express is housed should still be on your right as you turn onto this street.

Now that you're on via della Vigna Nuova, and away from the often hectic traffic, take a look at this corner residence, which was once home to the seventeenth-century Duke of Northumberland (or Sir "Roberto" Dudley as he was called in Florence). His aristocratic father, Sir Robert, Sr., the Earl of Leicester, was the acknowledged paramour of Queen Elizabeth I. For many years it was rumored that once Sir Robert, Sr., got rid of his heiress wife, Amy Robsart, he would marry the queen and wear the "Crown Matrimonial." The marriage between Robert and Amy, although legal, had never been officially blessed by the Church, or, understandably, by the British monarch. The hapless product of this union was little Robert, Jr., who was considered to be a nonentity if not a bastard. As Sir Robert spent most of his time around court, he banished Amy and their son to a secluded monastery near Oxford for practical reasons. One dark, gloomy day poor Amy was found dead with a broken neck from a mysterious fall down a flight of stairs. The official inquest was discreet and the question of foul play was never brought up, at least not in court. Most of England suspected Elizabeth's lover of having had a strong hand in the fall, and Elizabeth herself was not above suspicion in plotting the "accident."

The title-less son, Robert, Jr., grew up and made a name for himself in his native land as an accomplished military officer and navigator. Still, his family background prevented him from enjoying a prominent role in English society; in 1612, he took off for greener pastures in Italy. Cosimo II was impressed with the Englishman's naval experience, and he put him to work designing ships at Leghorn, a port along the western coast of Tuscany. In recognition of his contributions to the Grand Duchy, Cosimo created a title just for "Roberto": Duke of Northumberland and the Holy Roman Empire. The nobleman spent his last years in this splendid palace, and he was well received in the social world of the Medici court. He died in 1649, leaving various male descendants all over Europe with equally distinguished positions and titles to uphold.

To your left and across from the Duke of Northumberland's palace is a dark alleyway inauspiciously named via dell'Inferno. This little street makes an obvious reference to Dante's *Divine Comedy*, but it also serves as a warning of the worldly temptations that lie ahead of you along this fashionable boulevard.

Stop at no. 6 on the right side of the street and next door to the sleek boutique Ungaro. Over the front door to this modest fifteenth-century building is an unconventional architectural detail. The architrave, or molding, over the front door is covered with slender, carved lilies. (One of the heraldic symbols of Florence is the lily.) The three daggers superimposed over the field of lilies are the family coat of arms of the Minerbetti, the first residents of the palace. Before centuries of wear and tear, the daggers were enameled in white and the background behind the lilies was a crimson red.

Across the street, at no. 47/r, is the dress shop Valentino with a life-size brass "V" on the door.

At no. 45/r is Centrodisco, a newly opened record shop with a Florentine touch. Walk inside and see how patches of brick walls and parts of the vaulted ceiling from the original palace blend in with the stark white walls, coal-black shelves, silver turntables, red tubing, and shimmering neon lights.

At no. 53/r is Fantoni, a cluttered and cheerful ceramics store crammed with colorful hand-painted plates, dishes, mugs, and lamp bases. The proprietor is an amiable silver-haired lady who will sooner or later tell you (if you understand the basics of Italian) that her daughter is married to one of the famous ceramists of the Fantoni family. Their studios and kilns are located outside Florence and can be visited by appointment.

Halfway down via della Vigna Nuova, on the left, is an open square, Piazza Rucellai. There, to the right of the square, at no. 18, is an architectural wonder of Florence: Palazzo Rucellai, the first full-scale Renaissance palace in Italy. Designed in 1446 by Leon Battista Alberti for the wool-dyeing magnate Giovanni Rucellai, this imposing residence broke all the medieval rules of building and catapulted the Renaissance style of architecture to the fore.

Alberti's spacious rectangular palazzo efficiently replaced the clusters of family towers that were the motley medieval homes of the Florentines. The successful fifteenth-century merchant wanted to establish an image of solidity in finances, family, and home. The palazzo, or urban mansion, was the physical culmination of achievement in all three areas. An economic and political boost to the palazzo movement was the lengthy reign of Cosimo the Elder throughout the fifteenth century. For the longest period in its history so far, Florence began to enjoy a stable government and a prosperous business environment. Profits that would have been squandered on family defense funds against neighborly feuds were used to create more sumptuous living conditions. Throughout this century, over a hundred of these stone palaces, costing what would be millions of dollars each today, rose on the side streets around the center of old Florence.

Have a seat on one of the palace's cool stone benches if you're in the mood for a break from walking. The benches are of architectural interest in themselves. With the end of medieval family bickering, the Florentine merchants built benches facing the open piazzas in order to facilitate socializing away the cool summer nights. Gossip was exchanged, flirtatious invitations were extended, and marriages were negotiated on Renaissance palace benches. Machiavelli left this remembrance of bench-life in Florence:

> Girolamo del Guanto lost his wife and for three or four days acted as though he had been pole-axed; then he came back to life and wanted another wife, and we have been talking marriage each evening on the Capponi benches.

Take a look at the façade of the Rucellai Palace. The special touches designed by Alberti are what dictated future Renaissance style and taste.

Alberti measured and planned out every square inch of the façade. Symmetry and balance were his watchwords. The façade is sliced into three floors of equal height. Each floor is cut vertically by row upon row of pilasters, while the top line of each window bisects every rectangle made by the floor lines and pilasters.

Alberti used classical elements in a nonclassical way. He looped Roman arches around mullioned windows, and he played around with pilasters and capitals of various orders, which was virtually unheard of until the fifteenth century. The ground floor is a smooth-faced wall lined with pilasters topped with capitals of the Tuscan/Doric order. The second story was called the *piano nobile*, the nobleman's floor, because this was the quietest and coolest spot in the palace, and so it was where the head of the household worked and slept. The capitals over the pilasters are a composite of styles with a strong leaning toward the Corinthian. The top floor was the least comfortable level to live on. Servants and children were relegated to this area under the roof; it was unbearably hot in summer, drafty and

Rucellai Palace (via della Vigna Nuova 18)

chilly in winter. Corinthian-covered pilasters embellish the highest floor. The Rucellai family arms are displayed between the second and third floors to the left of the façade.

In one imaginative stroke, Alberti dictated the principles of the future Renaissance style: mathematical precision and classical ornamentation.

Across the piazza is Alberti's celebrated Rucellai Loggia. It's a large, detached three-arched veranda and a fifteenth-century descendant of the earlier thirteenth-century porches extended from medieval Florentine towers. The Rucellai Loggia is now one of the most chic art galleries in town and well worth investigating for the latest in contemporary Italian art. The policy of the gallery is to invite the artist or artists to "sit" for the shows, so if you wander around inside, be careful with your critical comments, whether in English or Italian!

Never could there have been a more fitting inhabitant of the first Renaissance palace than Giovanni Rucellai, textile and dye magnate and self-made aristocrat. Giovanni made a king's ransom in the textile business, and then lived like one. There was also no more grateful a citizen of the Renaissance capital. In his memoirs, Giovanni counts his blessings and revels in his good fortune at being "a Christian and not a Turk, Moor, or Tartar; and for having been born in Italy . . . and above all, in the city of Florence."

The consummation of Giovanni's success was the arranged marriage of his son, Bernardo, to Nannina, the niece of Cosimo and daughter of Piero de' Medici. The wedding date was set for June 8, 1466, and the pageantry involved was as splendid as was ever witnessed by Florentines, who were quite accustomed to the unusual and the extravagant.

Giovanni went all out on wedding decorations. Red and yellow silk was draped from the pilasters of each of the palazzo floors. A large triangular wooden platform was built in the center of the piazza in front of the loggia. A deep blue canopy tent was raised over the platform, and garlands of pink and ruby roses streamed down the sides of the tent. The Rucellais pulled out their most lavishly patterned Oriental rugs and tapestries and covered the platform, the piazza, and the benches with them. A block-long trestle table was moved to the side of the tent. The fifty or so servants scurried in and out of the palace covering the table with hundreds of capons, chunks of buffalo cheese, dozens of stuffed turkeys, plates of fresh fish caught in the Arno, tiny birds and hares, pies and tarts of pomegranates, baskets of soft cream cheese wrapped in mint leaves, and barrels of Greek as well as Italian wines.

The young Medici maiden arrived at the feast on horseback accompanied by the four highest-ranking politicians in Florence. Arrayed in a white velvet gown trimmed in pearls and gold-embroidered lace that flashed in the morning sunlight, the bride was as dazzling as the pageantry around her.

Giovanni entertained a constant flow of guests in the piazza from early Sunday morning until late Tuesday night. Banquets, concerts, acrobats, and jugglers attracted crowds of visitors up and down via della Vigna Nuova. As the final spectacle, on the last evening, the father of the bridegroom staged a flag-waving, trumpet-blaring jousting tournament. Hundreds of onlookers crowded into windows and onto balconies and rooftops to watch the start of the tournament in the Piazza Rucellai. The cavaliers and their steeds took off from the starting line in front of the palace door and battled their way down the via della Vigna Nuova to the intersection of via dei Tornabuoni.

Before making your right-hand turn onto via Palchetti, look up along the upper stories of the residence that's next door and to the left of Palazzo Rucellai. The *sgraffito* work etched on the façade is unusually ornate and in almost perfect condition except for some weathering around the edges.

Turn right between these two palaces, continue down via Palchetti a few yards, and stop at no. 4, a small side door to Palazzo Rucellai and the entrance to the four-hundred-year-old Compagnia del Paiolo or "Academy of the Cauldron." The narrow winding stairs behind this door will lead you to the third-floor galleries of Florence's oldest artistic society. Open from 5:30 P.M. to 8:00 P.M., the galleries display etchings, watercolors, pen-and-ink drawings, and oil paintings produced by the academy members. The original works are for sale in the $100-to-$250 range. Many of the exhibitors are professors of art and design in various universities in and around Florence. The English sculptor Henry Moore is a member in good standing, but don't look for any bargains among sculptures of his in the academy. Poets, novelists, and musicians round out the membership. Classical guitarist Andrés Segovia is another international celebrity who belongs to this circle.

The sixteenth-century members of the Academy of the Cauldron were an inventive bunch. The painters, sculptors, and architects gathered each month not to discuss each others' works but to enjoy a bacchanalian potluck dinner of elaborate proportions.

The name of the group was derived from the peculiar setting for the monthly dinners. Ordinary chairs and tables were not for these bohemians. Instead, everyone congregated inside an enormous copper vat that was more typically used for crushing grapes by a group of merry, barefoot peasants. Inside the vat was hung a tree with the widest and sturdiest branches that could be found. The dishes prepared by the members were attached to the branches, and the happy club wined and dined out of the tree while musicians on the outside of the vat serenaded the revelers with flutes and lyres. When the food from the branches was entirely consumed, the tree was lifted out of the vat by servants. More dishes were hooked onto the limbs and the tree was lowered down again.

The party dishes were as bizarre as the party locale. The artist-cooks tried to outdo each other with culinary creations of famous literary scenes, artistic tableaux, and architectural landmarks. The motif of the cauldron was often incorporated into the dishes. At one particularly memorable dinner, the founder of the academy, Giovanni Rustici, sculpted a large cauldron out of dough. He then dressed up two boiled capons, one as Ulysses, who was dunking the other capon, his father, into the pastry cauldron to rejuvenate him. Another artist, Roberto, decided that the cauldron needed an anvil for occasional repair work. He forged a one-of-a-kind anvil out of a meaty veal's head.

The sixteenth-century painter Andrea del Sarto, better known for his portraits of gentle Madonnas and saints, came up with the party's pièce de résistance. He constructed an eight-sided cake in the image of the Florentine Baptistery. The cake was placed on top of columns that appeared to be of porphyry but were, in reality, Parmesan cheese. The pavement around the octagonal church was a huge plate of multicolored gelatin that was molded to look like mosaics. The cornice of the temple was of sugared dough. Inside the cake was a marzipan altar and on the altar was a Bible-stand made of cold veal. The Bible was crafted out of thin layers of pasta with minuscule pepper-grain lettering. Surrounding the altar was a choir composed of open-beaked, stuffed thrushes. The choir was meticulously garbed in finely tailored pork skins.

Over the centuries the academy has relaxed its dinner customs. For many years the social events were held at the restaurant Il Latini, which you'll see downstairs and to the left of the academy entrance in via Palchetti. Nowadays the famous dinners are held in Piazza Santa Maria Novella at Il Girarrosta. The academy's credo is more food for thought:

> Those who are initiated
> into the Academy of the Paiolo

Via Palchetti

Want this and only this:
Who is talented should reveal themselves
And who is not, conceal themselves.

Turn left onto via del Moro. You're now passing through one of Florence's woodworking quarters. Most of the workshops are open to the street, and visitors are welcome to watch the works-in-progress. Florence's woodworking artisans are divided into two categories: antique restorers and antique counterfeiters. You'll see studios of both kinds of artisans along via del Moro and the upcoming street via del Porcellana.

Via del Moro runs into Piazza Goldoni. The square is named for the eighteenth-century Venetian playwright and father of Italian comedy, Carlo Goldoni. Have a seat on one of the park benches behind his smiling statue with the flowing cape.

The bridge to the left of the square is the Ponte alla Carraia, or "Bridge of the Cart Road." The first bridge on this spot was built in 1218. Monks who lived in the neighborhood of the Piazza Goldoni constructed a bridge to transport their manufactured woolen goods across the Arno.

In the spring of 1304 an open invitation went out around Florence: those who wished to receive a direct message from Satan and the underworld should gather on the Ponte alla Carraia for May Day. Hundreds of curious Florentines huddled onto this bridge in the evening while a band of actors dressed as devils sailed down the Arno in a barge. The craft halted under the bridge, and the devils began to act out a drama. More spectators pressed onto the bridge to view the fiendish sights. Suddenly the bridge collapsed, and the audience plunged into the river, where most of them rapidly joined the characters of the real underworld that night.

Floodwaters of the Arno destroyed the bridge several times, and the Germans, in 1944, blasted away at the nineteenth-century version of the Ponte alla Carraia. After World War II, the bridge as you see it now was rebuilt along the same lines as the nineteenth-century design.

Walk down Borgo Ognissanti, which is to your right and one block in from the river. On the right side of the street, 100 yards from Piazza Goldoni, is the Hospital of San Giovanni di Dio at no. 20. It was founded in 1400 by Simone Vespucci, a not-too-distant relation of Amerigo Vespucci, the fifteenth-century New World explorer. The territories that Amerigo claimed to have run across years before Columbus were then named the "Americas" after the Florentine explorer.

Stroll inside the opulent Baroque lobby, walk through the short hallway to the back, and continue either to the right or left along the sides of the open courtyard filled with palm trees and gardenia plants. In an alcove behind the courtyard are four murals showing scenes of the miraculous healings of San Giovanni; one painting depicts Christ ascending into the heavens. The panel facing the courtyard is of a flower-filled urn. A pomegranate is stuck in the center of the arrangement, and a cross appears to be sprouting from the fruit. The pomegranate and the cross were symbols of the Spanish city Granada. The Spanish friars who took over the administration of the hospital in the seventeenth century adopted the symbols as the logo for the hospital.

Again the 1966 flood has left its mark in what seems to be an inaccessible spot. Notice the lines of the

Macelleria ("butcher shop") (via del Porcellana and via Palazzuolo)

floodwaters on the paintings, and try to imagine what the splendid lobby and courtyard must have looked like at the time of that disaster.

Walk outside the hospital and stop next door at no. 22. This is the old Vespucci palace. The upper floors are now part of the hospital.

Turn right at this palace onto via del Porcellana. More woodworking shops abound along this block. Squeezed in between the studios on the left side of the street and to the right of the door marked no. 5 is Alpha Centauri, a small shop for the astrological enthusiast with expensive tastes. Everything from crystal balls to colorful Tarot cards is in stock at this elegant shop. Both French and Italian guidebooks to the stars are available here. Florentines have always had a weakness for access to the supernatural. Ever since the first century A.D. soothsayers from Fiesole and fortune-tellers from the Tuscan hillsides have ambled down to Florence and enjoyed a brisk and profitable business.

At via del Porcellana 25/r is the Trattoria Sostanza, and if you haven't succumbed to a lunch or dinner along this walk yet, don't overlook this seemingly modest restaurant. Celebrities of all nationalities head for via del Porcellana and the witty admonitions of

Mario, the headwaiter. (Queen Elizabeth's portrait painter, Anigoni, is often sitting at a corner table with an entourage of companions and fellow artists.) Mario is bilingually charming (Italian and English). While serving the broiled poultry dish of the house to a crowd of guests, he has been known to announce "These are the best breasts in Florence—chicken breasts, that is." Don't expect fanciness. Guests are seated at the white damask-cloth tables with other previously unacquainted guests, but after a few wine bottles are uncorked, conversations begin to flow. Virtually any dish is special at the Sostanza. This is the place to try *bistecca alla fiorentina*, and for dessert you'll want to sample a Tuscan treat: tiny wild strawberries soaked in a white wine sauce.

Next to the Sostanza, you'll spot an art restoration shop.

On the right-hand corner of via del Porcellana and via Palazzuolo is the Macelleria, a butcher shop in its (almost) original nineteenth-century state, complete with original tile work and butchers wearing what appear to be crisp white morning coats.

Along the next 25 yards past the shop are more woodworking studios to gaze into. When you come to the cross street via della Scala you can end our walk with a turn to the right and a people-watching rest on the benches or the grassy lawn of Piazza Santa Maria Novella.

Walk

4

The Artisans' Quarter

Starting Point: North side of the Ponte S. Trinità (between lungarno Corsini and lungarno Acciaiuoli)

Woodworking studios that cater to Arab sheikhs, boulevards lined with palazzos, bargain restaurants, and baroque street statues are the fare in this walk in the Oltr'arno, the residential and artisans' quarter across the Arno and away from the bustle of downtown Florence.

We're standing in front of the seventeenth-century statue of *Spring*, a seductively posed marble muse to the left of the Ponte S. Trinità at the northern entrance. Have a seat on the bridge behind the statue and read a brief introduction to the Oltr'arno.

The neighborhood we're about to walk through is a curious blend of extremes. Well into the fourteenth century it became apparent that central Florence was bursting at the seams. Markets, shops, warehouses, and block-long palaces had taken over every square inch of the city as we've seen it in the other walks. Florence's working class—artisans, laborers, and servants to the wealthy merchant families—was forced to move across the river where housing was makeshift, primitive, bleak, and crowded. At the same time the prospering merchant class was expanding. This new stratum of society also crossed the Arno in search of wide open spaces and plenty of building room. Scores of sumptuous palazzos were built next to alleyways and shabby tenement houses.

In 1549, Elenora of Toledo, wife of Cosimo I, purchased the Pitti Palace, which sits on a rolling hill in the southeastern half of the Oltr'arno. A jack-of-all-trades designer, Bartolomeo Ammannati, was hired to add massive wings to the palace, construct an impressive courtyard, and landscape the Boboli Gardens. As a related project, Ammannati was asked to design a commanding bridge as a fitting entrance to the new Medici court. The last three bridges on this spot had been washed away by floods.

Ammannati was an ardent admirer of Michelangelo's sculptures, in particular his Medici Chapel monu-

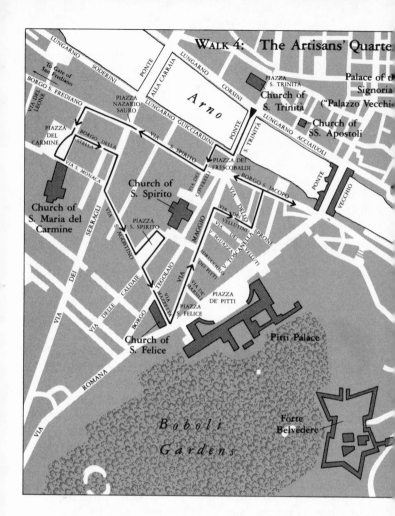

ments of *Day* and *Night* in the Basilica of San Lorenzo. Fascinated with Michelangelo's use of the *catenaria*, or "extended elliptical curve," in the design of the Medici sarcophagi, Ammannati decided to use the same form for the three arches that were to support the new bridge. Ammannati's bridge was blown up in the World War II bombing of Florence; the structure we're sitting on now is a reconstruction built in 1955–57. The elegant, simple, broad-spanned arches are naturally best seen from either of the two bordering bridges, the Ponte Vecchio or the Ponte alla Carraia.

The statues representing the four seasons at each corner of the bridge are the original sculptures that were added in 1608 when Cosimo II married Maria Maddalena of Austria. When the bridge was shelled in 1944, the statues were catapulted into the Arno River.

After the war, rescue teams were dispatched to the bottom of the Arno to retrieve the monuments. Every piece of all four statues was found with the exception of the head and right arm of *Spring*. The wildest of rumors circulated around Florence concerning the whereabouts of the head and arm. Antique shops were searched and one "witness" came forth with the story that he had seen an American soldier scurrying off with the head. Months later a New York newspaper reported that the head was spotted amidst the backyard greenery of a garden in Harlem. The assumptions and accusations came to an end in 1961 when another team of underwater investigators discovered the head resting in a mound of river mud under the Arno a few hundred yards from the bridge. The right arm was also recently recovered from the riverbed but as yet has not been repositioned.

The Arno still holds some twentieth-century Abstract Expressionist treasures for any adventurous divers to find. In 1952, the collagist and painter Robert Rauschenberg was putting together a collection of sculptural fantasies made of feathers, shells, pieces of cloth, wound rope, and mirrored boxes. A prestigious Florentine gallery invited him to show his "*scatole contemplative e feticci personali*," ("thought boxes and personal fetishes"), and the avant-garde artist arrived in town to set up the show. The day after the opening, a Florentine critic reported on Rauschenberg's curious objects: he declared them a "psychological mess." His advice to the American artist was to dump the disturbing pieces into the Arno. Rauschenberg read the review, and realizing that he was soon to leave Europe with little room in his luggage for the exhibit, decided to follow the critic's suggestion. When the show closed down, Rauschenberg collected the artworks, tied them up in a strong carton, and carried them down to the banks of the Arno. He looked around to make sure that no one on the road or along the river was nearby, and he heaved the collection into the Arno. No one to this day knows where the now priceless pieces are buried, and no one has reported discovering any strange aquatic artifacts from the river depths.

Walk along the right side of the bridge. At the end of the bridge cross the street, turn right, and walk 40

View of the Ponte alla Carraia as seen from the Ponte Santa Trinità

yards along the boulevard that runs parallel to the Arno, lungarno Guicciardini.

Watch for the small alleyway on the left that will be your turnoff, via dei Coverelli. This passageway comes right after the second palazzo to your left, a large terra-cotta-colored building marked no. 1.

While passing through via dei Coverelli, you can't help but notice the elaborately decorated wall on your right. The side of this palace was smoothed over with a thin layer of plaster and etched all over with cavorting cherubs, garlands of flowers, and bands of whimsical geometric shapes that look like a parade of Paul Klee figures. This is an example of the famous *sgraffito* work that was the last word in house decoration among the sixteenth-century Florentines. Take note of the arcade of plaster arches along the upper story of the wall. The *sgraffito* artist was attempting to imitate the stone arches that frame the massive windows of Renaissance palace façades. The plaster arches of this out-of-the-way passage enclose tiny attic windows that

are infrequently placed throughout the wall. The false brickwork is also intriguing. Every effort was made to give the appearance of the smooth, symmetrical masonry of a fifteenth-century palace, but the plaster peeling from twentieth-century pollution and traffic is beginning to wear away the imaginative effect.

At the end of via dei Coverelli is via Santo Spirito. Across the street from the *sgraffito* house, at nos. 5–7, is the former townhouse of Florentine statesman and political writer Niccolò Machiavelli. The *sporti*, or overhanging additions, to the house that jut out over via dei Coverelli were added in the fifteenth century. Machiavelli lived here in the late fifteenth through early sixteenth centuries while he served as a political adviser to and roving diplomat for the Florentine Republic. Out of grace with the Medici, who returned to political power in Florence in 1512, Machiavelli was forced to pack up and make his residence a poultry and produce farm on the outskirts of Florence.

Turn right down via Santo Spirito. At no. 40/r, about

100 yards down, is a compact antique store run by a young woman, Anna Bassi, who has a penchant for wrought-iron tools and pieces of architectural ornaments. Also for sale are foot-long metal keys that look like they might open any number of portals in a medieval castle.

Another 100 yards down via Santo Spirito on your right is Piazza Nazario Sauro. Keep walking straight ahead. What was once via Santo Spirito is now Borgo San Frediano. Up until the last twenty years or so Borgo San Frediano served as an informal dividing line between the palaces of the nobility we've just walked by and the true slums of Florence. A nineteenth-century visitor had this to say about the district: "Here live the lowest of the low classes of Florence."

The *borgo* today is a lively thoroughfare for traffic coming into and going out of the city. The neighborhood is residential but dotted with lively shops and restaurants. The population nowadays is generally made up of artisans, artists, shopkeepers, and students.

You'll be able to trace the scent of the shop Erborista yards away from its address at no. 16/r. Walk inside and sniff around the tissue-wrapped herbal soaps and teas and burlap bags of black henna.

Behind the polished wooden doors of no. 26/r is the popular and inexpensive trattoria Antica Cantina Capponi. The dining area is in the cellar, away from street noise and kitchen heat. In true trattoria style, you'll share tables with other guests. The restaurant is closed every Tuesday.

Walk 30 yards past the trattoria and stop in front of the broad, open Piazza del Carmine on your left. As you turn into the piazza to your right look down the *borgo* and you'll see the large, sandy-colored arch of the fourteenth-century Porta San Frediano ("Gate of San Frediano").

It was through this gate, in 1494, that Charles VIII, king of France, made his splendid entrance into Florence. Borgo San Frediano was packed solid with spectators when, on November 17 at 2:00 in the afternoon, the king arrived with a retinue of soldiers the likes of which the Florentines had never dreamed. One onlooker left this account:

> Charles went forward under a rich canopy.... On each side of him rode the Cardinals.... The royal body-guard

followed, consisting of a hundred knights of France on foot ... then came the Swiss Guard. . . . But the most splendid appearance of all was made by the cavalry: they had engraved armour, mantles of the richest brocade, banners of velvet embroidered with gold, chains of gold, and ornaments of the same precious metal.

The cuirassiers presented a hideous appearance with the horses looking like monsters, from their ears and tails cut short. The archers were extraordinarily tall men; they came from Scotland and other northern countries, and they looked more like wild beasts than men.

At Borgo San Frediano 33/r there's a pleasant trattoria with a plant-filled outdoor dining area facing the Piazza del Carmine.

Reigning over the square is the Church of Santa Maria del Carmine, a vast medieval stone structure with an unimposing, almost drab façade. The founders of the thirteenth-century church and monastery were the Carmelite friars whose order originated on Mount Carmel in Palestine. The stark, barnlike façade is deceiving. Walk inside and you'll come upon polished marble floors, glistening candles, and to the right of the altar, some of the most famous paintings in Renaissance art: the fifteenth-century frescoes of the Brancacci Chapel. Felice Brancacci, a prosperous Florentine merchant, politician, and neighborhood chieftain, hired as fresco painters Masolino and his pupil Masaccio to cover the chapel walls with scenes from Saint Peter's life. Two panels they painted that do not depict scenes of the saint's life are *Original Sin* by Masolino in the upper right corner and *Expulsion from Paradise* by Masaccio in the opposite left corner.

Notice the difference in style between the master, Masolino, and his apprentice, Masaccio. Both artists studied the works of architect and sculptor Brunelleschi, who was busy experimenting with light and shadow in an effort to create movement, depth, and emotion in his art forms. Brunelleschi's innovative techniques with line and perspective were to serve as the foundation of the principles of fifteenth-century Renaissance painting.

When Masolino set out to paint his *Original Sin*, however, he chose to ignore these new techniques. In his rendition of Adam and Eve, the older artist stuck to the more traditional methods. His figures are frontally

placed, statically posed, and evenly colored. Masolino's nude figures are elegant, calm, and controlled,
but no sense of mystery or complexity is introduced
into the story of his fresco.

Masaccio, on the other hand, painted *Expulsion
from Paradise* with all the artistic drama that he could
muster. Following Brunelleschi's methods, Masaccio
filled his fresco with dramatic shading, contorted lines,
and expressive body movements. The small wall painting comes alive with the emotions of the enlightened
but doomed couple in a way that earlier painters
would never have imagined possible.

Adam and Eve were not the only couple moved by
passion at the altar of the Brancacci Chapel. In his
Autobiography, Benvenuto Cellini remembers discussing his profound admiration for the incomparable Michelangelo Buonarroti with another sculptor and
influential colleague, Piero Torrigiano. The latter then
proceeds to provide Cellini with a little-known anec-
dote concerning his boyhood friendship with the artistic genius:

> This Buonarroti and I used to go along together when we
> were boys to study in Masaccio's chapel in the Church of
> the Carmine. Buonarroti had the habit of making fun of
> anyone else who was drawing there, and one day he pro-
> voked me so much that I lost my temper more than usu-
> al, and, clenching my fist, gave him such a punch on the
> nose that I felt the bone and cartilage crush like a biscuit.
> So that fellow will carry my signature till he dies.

Cellini, who was no pacifist himself, was so outraged
at this account that he immediately broke all ties with
the pugilist.

As you walk back down the aisle toward the front
entrance, look for an open door to your left. This will
be the passage to the seventeenth-century cloister of
the church. (The cloister area is promptly closed after
1:00 P.M.) Stroll around the vaulted hall or portico that
encircles the garden and well of the monastery. Simple
Doric capitals top the colonnade along the edge of the
walkway. Several stucco- and stone-walled rooms extend off the cloister. Walk into the first room along the
south wall, opposite the exit, and you'll find yourself
in a small-scale permanent exhibit entitled "*Come
nasce un affresco*," "How a fresco is born." The step-
by-step procedures and do's and don'ts of fresco-mak-

ing are explained with visual aids and English translations.

Helpful hints and secrets from the past masters are also revealed. For the first layer of plaster applied to the wall surface, Cennino Cennini, a fourteenth-century fresco artist, prescribed the use of *la calce* ("lime") that's *ben grassa e fresca* ("very fat and fresh"). The second layer of plaster, the *intonaco*, was troweled down to a glasslike smoothness according to the tastes of the earliest band of fresco painters, Cimabue, Giotto, and Michelangelo. Later sixteenth-century artists preferred a rougher, grainier look. Giotto's method of coating his faces with a bright green pigment before applying the flesh colors is illustrated with startling effect. The next time that you wander into the Peruzzi and Bardi chapels in the Church of Santa Croce you may want to remember that behind the serene visages of Giotto's saints are eerie, Martian-colored creatures.

Next door to the fresco exhibit is the refectory of the monastery. Painted on the wall is Alessandro Allori's *Last Supper*, which was completed in 1582.

In the room adjacent to the refectory is a miniature museum filled with panels, paintings, and pieces of old frescoes. Fra Filippino Lippi's painting *Confirmation of the Order* is on display. Lippi, a fifteenth-century monk who also worked on the frescoes in the Brancacci Chapel, was born and grew up a block away from the church.

When you're outside the main entrance of the church again, walk halfway through the piazza and turn right into the small side street, Borgo della Stella. Pass through this narrow byway with its gold-painted and occasionally ivy-covered stone wall on the left and woodworking studios on the right and you'll end up on via dei Serragli, another bastion of imposing palazzos, one right after another.

Turn right and continue past the small antique shops on your right.

Across the street at no. 17 is the art gallery Fratelli Paoletti ("Paoletti Brothers"), housed in the old palace of the Dati family, a well-to-do Florentine clan of "new money." We'll run across the original home of the family a few blocks farther along this walk. A lively literary society met here every week in the sixteenth century; they called themselves the "Società Cuculiana" ("The

Via dei Serragli

Cuckoolike Society"). The name was not total whimsy on their part. Around the corner from the palace, where you will turn left from via dei Serragli to via Sant'Agostino, is the Canto alla Cuculio or "Corner of the Cuckoo." Another very ancient Florentine family, the Velluti (whose property we'll also cross later), owned gardens at this spot, where a collection of cuckoos was once in residence.

Make a left turn at the Corner of the Cuckoo. This is via Sant'Agostino, Main Street to the small-town side of Florence. You'll pass by trucks unloading vegetables in front of a family grocery store, a barber shop packed with gossiping customers and children leafing through comic books in front of a closet-size secondhand bookstore.

At no. 8, 100 yards down on the left side of the street, is a solid, red-brick and rusticated stone struc-ture. The entablature over the door looks as weathered as a Greek ruin. This is the nineteenth-century Bagno Comunale or "Public Baths," a memorial to the simpler living conditions in the Oltr'arno. A not-too-dated sign on the front wall states that a bath will set you back 250 lire (about 30 cents) while the added luxury of soap and towel is 350 lire. The Public Baths have been in a state of continuous restoration for the last two years, so don't get your hopes too high for a look inside or a quick shower along the way.

Coming up on your left is the Piazza Santo Spirito. Set back behind the tree-lined square and the statue of the nineteenth-century agronomist Cosimo Ridolfi is the white-faced Church of Santo Spirito.

Both the piazza and the church were built in response to the fifteenth-century urban needs of this working-class quarter of Florence. Throughout the century the laboring population of the Oltr'arno expanded and spilled over into the already crowded nooks and crannies of the neighborhood. Wide-open public space for marketing, meetings, merrymaking, and meditating was badly needed. Unlike the irregular medieval squares that grew up haphazardly along the fringes of parish churches, the Piazza Santo Spirito was a deliberate act of urban planning. Tenements were torn down, and the spacious rectangular square that you see today was opened as a mall for the general populace.

Whether you're passing through the piazza in the morning hours or on a sunny afternoon or a balmy evening, you'll see the square filled with most of the same activities that have been going on here for the last five hundred years. A caravan of produce and low-priced clothing merchants are camped out under green-and-white striped umbrellas. Children are whirling about with balls, sticks, and makeshift vehicles created out of vegetable crates and broken bicycle wheels. (A plaque posted on the wall to the left of the piazza and dated 1639 announces an ordinance against ball playing in front of the church.) Benches are lined with senior citizens, young mothers, and politicos.

Piazza Santo Spirito, true to its earliest working-class heritage, is socialist territory. All summer long civic festivals of every persuasion are held in the square. On any given day, you may be wading through flapping banners that read *"Contra la violenza alle donne"* ("Against violence toward women"), *"Dove c'e violenza non c'e pace"* ("Where there is violence there is no peace"), and *"Ora e sempre pace"* ("Now and always peace").

Outdoor photographic exhibits of local restoration projects are often displayed on portable wood partitions.

Committees for promotion of environmental affairs frequently take over the piazza and decorate the corners with boldly printed posters written in English: "Save our Trees!" and "Water is Life!"

Background music to these street fairs and displays is invariably American—rock music blaring out of stereo amplifiers scattered around the square.

Piazza Santo Spirito is also an informal gathering place for students, Florentine and foreign, and their motorcycles. Occasional vendors of marijuana and other more exotic stimulants can also be spotted milling around the fountain. If you don't look particularly interested in their wares, you won't be approached.

The original settlers on this spot were thirteenth-century hermits from the order of Saint Augustine. The land under and around the church had been cultivated as a vineyard by the Velluti family (of the Corner of the Cuckoo). With the help of daily begging and neighborly donations, the hermits bought the vineyard and built a small monastery and church outside the gardens. As the population in the Oltr'arno expanded, the hermits' tiny church proved unsatisfactory. The congregants looked enviously across the river at the vast, showy churches of Santa Croce and Santa Maria Novella and decided to finance an equally impressive structure smack in the middle of the quarter. In 1428 Filippo Brunelleschi was hired to design the church. His original plan was to have the building face boldly out over the Arno toward the center of old Florence. The noble families who had already claimed the riverside real estate on this side of town didn't want the imposing church overshadowing their property, and they put a stop to this scheme. So the church was built with its back to their palazzos. Brunelleschi's death in 1446 temporarily interrupted construction. Finally, in 1487, the church was completed. The façade is noticeably simple. This is the way that Brunelleschi wanted it, and despite a brief but aborted plan in 1792 to jazz it up with sculptures and marble mosaics, the residents

Church of Santo Spirito

of the Santo Spirito neighborhood like it and want to keep it this way.

At the height of the Renaissance, the church provided the quarter with more than a sense of pride and beauty. Libraries, a school, a hospital, and a dormitory for pilgrims were added onto the worship area. The building complex of the fifteenth-century church of Santo Spirito grew into a scholarly retreat, social services center, and an oasis for wandering wayfarers. Martin Luther enjoyed the hospitalities of the church while en route to Rome on a business trip as a young Augustinian monk.

If you have a moment step inside for another first-hand experience with Florentine art history. Walk in through the main entrance and count the first fourteen paintings along the right wall. Stop in front of the fifteenth painting, which is under the cupola of the church. This is the famous panel of neighborhood artist Filippino Lippi, *Madonna Enthroned and Saints with Tanai de' Merli and his Wife*.

After Masaccio's early death at age twenty-eight, Lippi was commissioned to finish off the frescoes in the Brancacci Chapel of the Church of the Carmine. This assignment kept him busy between 1481 and 1485. Although he was working at close range with Masaccio's eloquent figures, Lippi made no effort to imitate his predecessor's style. Lippi developed his own sense of drama in his paintings with the use of imaginative compositions, intriguing backgrounds, and meticulously drawn details. The painting in front of us shows Lippi at his most florid. The beauteous Madonna is surrounded by the opulently clothed saints Catherine and Nicholas, the infant Jesus, young Saint John the Baptist, patron saint of Florence, and in the lower left- and right-hand corners, the patrons of the painting, Tanai de' Merli, a moneyed Florentine merchant, and his wife. Fat-cheeked cherubs gaze down at the scene from the flowing arched loggia of a lavish palace interior. Beyond the open windows are the western hills of Florence. Framed by the arch to the right of the Madonna is the massive Gate of San Frediano that we passed on our walk a while back.

Lippi's extravagant use of perspective and his stylish arrangement of figures were standard in Florentine painting by the close of the fifteenth century. The Mannerist form of art that developed in the next two centuries was a direct descendant of some of what we see here. Perspective was carried to an extreme. Painters created figures floating in space with no attempt to tie them down to a baseline. The fifteenth-century relish for theater turned into a sixteenth- and seventeenth-century taste for a restless, confusing array of bodies that splash over canvases with nervous, unfocused energy.

Back outside on the corner of the piazza and via Sant'Agostino (no. 2/r) is the trattoria Oreste. In warm weather you'll want to eat outside under the canopy and watch the goings-on in the square. The prices are reasonable, and many Florentines have midday dinner here. Try *coniglio arrosto* ("roasted rabbit") if you haven't tasted it yet.

Before leaving Piazza Santo Spirito we'll pause in front of two palaces that overlook the square.

Directly across from the statue of Ridolfi, at no. 12, is the fifteenth-century family seat of the Dati family and residence of Gregorio Dati, a self-made tycoon in the wool and silk business. Details of his private and business life are better known than those of most Florentine Renaissance merchants. Dati left a diary of his financial transactions, household arrangements, and intermittent business excursions. What emerges from his writings is the picture of a frugal, temperate lifestyle: his conservative exploits in money-making, discreet accumulation of property, and careful accounting of funds for the costly dowries of half a dozen unmarried daughters.

Grandson to a purse-maker whose shop on the Ponte Vecchio was swept away by a flood in 1333, Dati more than managed to keep his head above water. Early on in life he borrowed a substantial sum of money and embarked on a career as a merchant in the Florentine textile business. Buying and selling fabrics at a healthy profit, he was able to open a wool cloth shop, acquire a silk factory, and set up partnerships with trading companies in France and Spain. Eight houses in the Santo Spirito area and three working farms were purchased. Dati looked as if he would be living on easy street for the rest of his life when suddenly, in his later years, he was vexed with unexpected snags in his business operations. A series of pirate raids, plagues, wars, shipwrecks, and princes who ignored invoices contributed to the merchant's unforeseen bankruptcy when he was on the verge of retiring. But Dati's brother was the hero of the day. He extended a sizable and welcome loan to the business, and Dati started all over again rebuilding his textile empire.

Dati's diaries tell us one curious fact about his life as a Florentine merchant and resident of the Santo Spirito quarter: he was totally oblivious to the flourishing activities of building, frescoing, sculpturing, and painting in the churches of his neighborhood quarter. He quite obviously noticed the construction of the Church of Santo Spirito (it was right in his front yard) but as for any comments, passing thoughts, or curiosity about this cultural addition to his surroundings, Dati made no note in his diaries. Gene Brucker, in his introduction to a translation of Dati's diaries, makes this observation about the lack of interest in art by the Florentine merchants of this time:

Only if Brunelleschi or Masaccio had been employed to build or decorate their family chapel would they have described their artistic accomplishments. . . . Renaissance Florence was inhabited by individuals who, like most men at most times, placed the greatest importance upon visible, tangible material objectives, and who thought first of themselves and their own interests.

At the corner of the square, to your left as you face no. 12 and the juncture of Piazza Santo Spirito (no. 10) and via Mazzetta, is the famed fifteenth-century Palazzo Guadagni. This roomy palace is always a stopping-off point for architecture enthusiasts. The arched windows and upper-story loggia are perfect specimens of Renaissance domestic architecture in its best state of preservation. The architect, Simone del Pollaiolo, also worked on the designs for the sacristy and cloister of the Church of Santo Spirito. The Guadagni family dates back in the city records to 1204.

Don't leave the palace without examining the handsome wrought-iron lantern, or *fanale*, that's hanging from the corner of the mansion facing via Mazzetta. To display a finely crafted lantern such as this one was a symbol of status in Renaissance days but a symbol of status that went beyond just being able to pay the sizable bill. Permission to exhibit a lantern was granted by the city fathers only to those citizens who had performed extraordinarily heroic deeds or who were able to grease a few political palms. Amerigo Vespucci, on his return from having "discovered" the North American continent, was allowed to hang up a pair of lanterns outside his door. The Strozzi family, whose magnificent palace graces midtown Florence, hired the blacksmith Niccolò Grosso to forge four lanterns and numerous iron rings to adorn their home. There is an interesting story of family rivalry that circulates around Florence concerning this commission. The Strozzi built their fortresslike, stone-lined palace as a testimony to their supreme social prominence in Florentine society. Then, along came the Pitti family, who had the funds and the room to construct a much larger residence in the Oltr'arno (now the Pitti Palace). They also had the audacity to announce openly at frequent social gatherings that the Strozzi Palace would fit into a small wing of their family house! The Strozzi didn't take this lying down. They immediately began to work their way through the proper bureaucratic circles to procure the right to decorate their palace with the coveted lanterns and rings.

The existence of the Guadagni lantern is probably due more to financial strength than fortitude on the battlefield or the high seas. As a matter of fact, one Bernardo Guadagni, who had a high government post, was instrumental in exiling Cosimo de' Medici in 1433. Upon his return to Florence a year later, however, Cosimo kidnapped Bernardo's son and had him publicly beheaded.

The street across from the palace is via delle Caldaie, "Street of the Boilers." This is one of the old medieval quarters where the dye-making for wool fabrics took place.

As you turn left onto via Mazzetta, glance up at the corner of the palace wall that is farthest from the piazza. You'll see one of the massive wrought-iron rings that were used to prop up banners and to hitch horses. You've undoubtedly spotted smaller rings like this one in walls of buildings all over Florence, but this piece of hardware is unusually large and rare.

About 25 yards from the Guadagni Palace is Borgo Tegolaio, which cuts across via Mazzetta. This street was the old tile-making center of Florence. The principal product of this block was the terra-cotta-colored roofing tiles that you still see all over Florence. Clay for the tiles was wedged and molded in workshops in Borgo Tegolaio on the left side of via Mazzetta. The slabs of unfired tiles were then carted across via Mazzetta to the section of the *borgo* on your right. This part of the street was where the unfinished tiles were stacked in wood-burning *fornaci*, or "kilns," that were installed in more pottery studios.

At the end of via Mazzetta is the Piazza San Felice. On your right is the eleventh-century Church of San Felice. Owned and operated by monks for the first four hundred years of its existence, the church was then taken over by Dominican nuns. In 1552 the sisters set up a shelter here for runaway wives.

The fifteenth-century palazzo on the left side of the street at the corner of via Mazzetta and via Maggio is the literary landmark Casa Guidi, home for thirteen years to the Victorian poets Elizabeth Barrett and Robert Browning. The romantic couple began to set up housekeeping in Florence in 1848 for practical and professional reasons. Elizabeth's father had forbidden both his male and female offspring from entering into the questionable state of marriage. His celebrated daughter's elopement with a then-obscure poet was not met with wild enthusiasm in the Moulton-Barrett household, and the couple thought that a residence in Italy might prove more conducive to preserving familial harmony. Elizabeth and Robert were also Italophiles in the most ardent sense. Elizabeth wrote back to a friend in England: ". . . there is no place like Florence . . . cheap, tranquil, cheerful, beautiful, within the limits of civilization, yet out of the crush of it." Robert was more introspective about the town: "I felt alone with my soul there."

Casa Guidi was the perfect refuge for the Brownings, and their most productive years as poets were spent at this corner in Florence. The location provided them with a source of inspiration.

Contrary to the legendary image of her as a languid, long-suffering invalid, Elizabeth was a visibly prominent social figure in and around Florence for the first five years of her life here. In the next eight years, until her death in 1861, she was less physically active but very much intellectually curious and creative. Elizabeth was also passionately interested in politics. She found herself caught up in one of the most dramatic chapters in the history of Italy, the "Risorgimento," the political struggle devoted to the unification of all Italy under one government. Elizabeth's fascination with the intrigues and events around her was all-consuming. She devoured newspapers, conferred with visiting dignitaries, clattered around town in a horse-drawn carriage, and surveyed military parades from the small overhang that we see directly above us on via Mazzetta.

The poetess was vehemently opposed to oppression of any kind, a passion that may have evolved from her strained relations with an opinionated father. She revered Harriet Beecher Stowe for her stand against slavery, encouraged women to pursue the highest educational ideals (Elizabeth herself read in seven languages), and denounced organized religions—Protestant and Catholic—for undue pomp and aristocratic arrogance. What she saw around her was a battle by

neighboring countries for bits and pieces of her beloved adopted homeland, and she felt that it was only
a matter of time before Florentines would be forced to
salute a foreign flag of one nationality or another. Elizabeth's response to this crisis was to write a poem, and
the result of this effort was an epic verse entitled "Casa
Guidi Windows." In this work the poet chose the image of a small neighborhood boy as the symbol of her
hope of unification and freedom for future Italians.
The first lines begin:

> I heard last night a little child go singing
> 'Neath Casa Guidi windows, by the church,
> "O bella libertà, O bella!" . . .
> . . . And that the heart of Italy must beat,
> While such a voice had leave to rise serene
> 'Twixt church and palace of a Florence street.

Elizabeth mailed the manuscript off to the prestigious British literary magazine *Blackwood*. The editor
promptly returned the verses with a rejection slip and
an admonition that women writers should stick to
their more familiar role of "adorning the domestic circle" and forget about any opinions of "cosmopolitanism." "Casa Guidi Windows" has since survived many
printings elsewhere. Elizabeth Barrett Browning died
in Casa Guidi in 1861 when virtually all of Italy was
joined under one unified government with the exceptions of Venice and Rome.

Robert Browning was also moved to write about the
view from the Casa Guidi terrace. In his poem "The
Ring and the Book" he describes a restless, feverish
feeling he contracts after reading a trashy murder mystery that he found in a downtown Florentine book-
stall. Browning writes that to relieve his preoccupation
with the sordid story, he walked out on the terrace for
a breath of fresh air:

> I turned to free myself and find the world,
> And stepped out on the narrow terrace, built
> Over the street and opposite the church,
> And paced its lozenge-brickwork sprinkled cool . . .

The exhilaration of the great outdoors abates the poet's feverishness, and he begins to reflect on the
church, its windows, and the celestial-sounding sing-
ing nuns inside:

Because Felice-church-side stretched, a-glow
Through each square window fringed for festival,
Whence came the clear voice of the cloistered ones
Chanting a chant made for midsummer nights—
I know not what particular praise of God,
It always came and went with June.

Browning was even more completely brought back to reality with the sight of happy-go-lucky mortals strolling through the street:

Beneath . . .
I' the street . . .
The townsmen walked by twos and threes, and
    talked,
Drinking the blackness in default of air—
A busy human sense beneath my feet.

After Elizabeth's death, Browning and his son, "Penino" ("Little Feather"), lived on only a short while at Casa Guidi. They returned to England, where Browning was less active poetically but busier socially. He finished his years as a welcome guest at the court of Queen Victoria, the darling of the popular Browning Society, and the ex-suitor of Lady Ashburton, who sued him for a late-in-life breach of promise. "Penino" Browning followed in his father's footsteps romantically but not literarily.

Make a left turn around the corner of Casa Guidi. Rolled out in front of you like a royal red carpet is via Maggio, a wealthy residential street little changed since the heyday of the great Renaissance merchant princes. Via Maggio, on both sides of the street, is lined with palazzos. The only twentieth-century touches to these mansions are the elegant, softly lit window displays along the street. The ground floors to these palazzos are now some of the poshest antique stores, art galleries, auction houses, and flower shops in Florence.

Before forging ahead you may want to mull over the possibility of a meal at the trattoria Le Quattro Stagioni at no. 61/r. Their food and wine list are slightly higher priced than the usually modest restaurants on this side of the Arno, but Florentines from the neighborhood don't seem to mind spending the extra lire. Dinners at noon are especially lively. Take a corner table and enjoy the good food and good humor of the staff and clientele.

You may also want to read ahead a bit about the history of via Maggio and its architectural scenery.

In the medieval days of the thirteenth and fourteenth centuries, the wool business of Florence, the principal source of income for the town, made its corporate headquarters in the wide thoroughfare of via Maggio. The street's name comes from *majus* ("wide") because it was originally the widest road in Florence. Sixty wool shops carried on the hectic production, sale, and transportation of fabrics in this centrally located, very accessible spot in the Oltr'arno. At the end of via Maggio is Ponte S. Trinità, which stretches out over the Arno and links up with the well-traveled boulevard of via Tornabuoni and downtown Florence.

In fact, via Maggio was so ideally situated that by the middle of the fourteenth century the Renaissance merchants who were raking in the profits from wool decided to build homes along the street. Most of the small two- and three-story shops were torn down and bulwarklike palaces were built over what once had been the space of five or six businesses. By the mid-sixteenth century only five wool shops had survived what was to be the biggest building boom in Florentine history.

Between the late fourteenth and early sixteenth centuries, well over a hundred spacious stone-faced palaces were built all around Florence. The Renaissance palazzo craze was born of a change of mood among the upwardly mobile Florentine merchants. By the end of the fourteenth century no self-respecting successful businessman wanted to live in an apartment over his shop or even rent out the open porch on the ground floor of his house. As the shrewd and thrifty textile merchants began to accumulate kingly fortunes, they also decided to shed all outward signs of their crass commercial lives and live more like affluent, aloof princes of state. Hawking and selling and general business affairs conducted in the street were now considered vulgar in respectable residential neighborhoods. Any architectural features that were suggestive of this former way of life were completely covered up. On some late thirteenth- or early fourteenth-century buildings around Florence you'll see the outlines of stone arches along the top of the ground floor. Under these arches were once open porches where produce, crafts, and fabrics were sold. Bricks and plaster were used to block up these early Renaissance storefronts, and the houses were made to look as if they had been built solely for living purposes.

At the same time, another everyday human activity was being banished from the streets. Well-to-do Florentines no longer thought it fitting for them to sit out on the family loggia, which extended out over the street and served as an informal warm-weather living room. The old loggias, such as the Cerchi loggia on the first walk, were walled up, and Florentines stopped socializing from the doorstep and people-watching from behind the shade of a cool arch. Everyone—the merchant, the mistress of the house, the maidservants—moved inside, closed the shutters, and shut the door. A new era of living in houses had begun.

The Renaissance palazzo was designed with two social gains in mind: family privacy on the inside and an awesome image on the outside. Interclan feuds in the street and making a fast buck in the open market square were customs of the barbaric, medieval past. Scandalous, interesting things still happened in the rational, scientific days of the fifteenth-century Renaissance, but they somehow all took place behind heavy, ornately carved closed doors.

As you stroll down via Maggio, you'll be able to detect architectural evidence of the new Renaissance upper-class life. One feature that's hard to miss on these palatial residences is the oversized arched entranceway. Many of the doors look as if they were created for a herd of elephants to pass through. The extreme size of these front doors was an intentional social symbol to the passerby. With the removal of all outward signs of business from the housefront, the Renaissance home-owner now wanted to emphasize that his home was a residence and a residence only. By having a single, central door so obviously hard to overlook, the palazzo dweller was also telling the world that one family lived here and not a conglomeration of produce salesmen, extraneous relatives, and paying lodgers who would have required several doors at various locations around the house.

Each proud owner of these palaces also wanted to

express his individuality. The basic construction of the palaces varies little. On the exterior, they're rectangularly shaped, and three or four stories tall. Inside, the rooms of each palazzo encircle a central courtyard complete with immaculately tended gardens and at least one well for drinking and washing. The more elaborate palaces had overhanging terraces around the courtyard and stables, and had a carriage room.

As the interior of the palazzo was strictly a private area reserved for family and a few close friends, the only obvious spot on the house that could be used for impressing the general populace was the street façade. When the Florentine family moved out of the street-level loggia and into the palazzo courtyard for outdoor living pleasure, they left behind an architectural memento on the front wall. The family crest or coat of arms carved in stone was conspicuously hung over the front door or at a conspicuous corner of the house. The façade itself was often decorated to the hilt. The Renaissance palace dweller had a reasonable variety of decorative choices.

One popular effect for façade ornamentation was rustication. Palace residents liked the idea of appearing to live within a fortified castle. You'll notice that many street-level floors of the palazzos are covered with rough-surfaced blocks of stone outlined by clearly cut beveled edges that create a highly textured and symmetrical patterning in the wall. Some façades are simply plastered over, and stonework is used to frame arched windows and to decorate the edges of the house. Finally, as tastes became more elaborate and home-owners more anxious to outdo each other, the art of frescoing façades, or *sgraffito*, came into fashion. Along all of these walks, you've seen some palazzos with delicate plaster etchings of flowers and cherubs splashed over the outside walls.

The Florentine palazzo that carries façade decoration to sublime heights is at via Maggio 26. This is the former residence of Bianca Cappello, mistress and eventual wife of Francesco de' Medici, Grand Duke of Tuscany in the early sixteenth century. (Turn to pages 126–28 for more specific details about how Bianca came into possession of this palace.) The *sgraffito* work on Bianca's house is particularly florid and detailed. The upper floors of this fanciful abode look as if they've been wallpapered in expensive Belgian lace. Most of the *sgraffito* in good condition around Florence consists of thin bands and friezes above the front door or between floors; it's unusual to see the greater part of the façade covered with such embellishments. Bianca was evidently a woman who had little interest in moderation. Look above the door and you'll see an architectural pun on the former owner's name: Bianca's surname, Capello, translates into "hat," and this piece of apparel (in stone) is exactly what tops off the architrave over the front door.

Bianca lived here in those delicate years when she was a close companion to the duke but not at liberty to marry him because his wife was still quite healthy. The duke's house, luckily, was only a stone's throw away from Bianca's; he was living over on the next block at the Pitti Palace. A fascinating rumor still circulates that an underground tunnel was constructed between Bianca's house and some remote chambers in the Pitti Palace, but Florentine archaeologists have as yet not tackled this tantalizing project.

Across the street from Bianca's house and a few yards ahead is via de' Velluti; pass it, and continue walking another few yards to the next narrow passage known as via dei Vellutini. We will turn right at this small street. Before walking through it you may want to have a glance at the palazzo of the Velluti family, the original landowners of a large part of the area we cover in this walk. You may remember that a short while back we passed through their property in via dei Serragli, via Sant'Agostino, and Piazza Santo Spirito. Their family house is at via Maggio 9.

In the early twelfth century Buonaccorso Velluti bought up the property that via Maggio crosses through now. He cleared the land, planted crops, and cut a small road through his fields so that he could cart his vegetables into the city. Over the centuries via Maggio grew into a strategic shopping and business center for the Oltr'arno, and the Velluti descendants simply sat back and collected the rent checks. The Palazzo Velluti is a typical early Renaissance home—with one exception. You'll notice right away that there are two front doors instead of the usually grandiose one. The palace originally had one large door for one small-sized family. When the father of a branch of the Velluti family died, two of the sons inherited the house and they both decided to live here, each with his own family. The rooms were divided up, new walls were built that sliced up lofty salons and hallways, and two front doors were built into the façade. This was the beginning of the two-family palazzo.

The twentieth-century fate of these mansions has seen an ironic turnabout. Originally constructed as statements about a family's wealth, the palazzos have since been chopped up and restructured into mazes of apartments, offices, and high-rent artists' studios. The ground floors, which once included stables, garden rooms, storage areas, and offices for the master of the house, are now showrooms for the genteel commercial enterprises that you see along the street. And so, the palazzos today have more of a resemblance to the hodgepodge medieval structures than all the structures that were meant to replace them. Unrelated occupants with a variety of pursuits live side by side in the former mansions while business as usual is conducted downstairs in the smart shops overlooking via Maggio.

When you turn down the narrow passage of via dei Vellutini, you'll be entering one of the oldest woodworking quarters in the Oltr'arno. Read a page or so ahead before continuing down this small street.

The Renaissance palaces we've just seen along via Maggio were a result of the demand for more spacious family living. The new palace floor plan called for rooms that were large and numerous. When the wealthy Renaissance merchants and their families moved into these mansions, they found themselves rambling around labyrinths of private chambers, hidden alcoves, long hallways, and stately living rooms. These rooms were impressive but empty. Before moving into these mansions, Renaissance families had made do with few possessions. Clothes were stored in a couple of medieval chests; meals were eaten on benches around a simple wooden table; nights were passed in unornamented beds. Now the families discovered that these palaces had to be filled up with all kinds of trappings and trinkets.

A new market opened up and quick-thinking businessmen, penniless artists, and energetic salesmen answered the call of opportunity. A flood of carved furniture, gilded candelabra, painted pottery, embroidered curtains, mass-produced murals, marble statues, silk tapestries, and suits of armor came pouring out of hastily set-up workshops. The flood of gewgaws went right into the cavernous palazzos. Florentine craftsmanship had really begun, and it took off for a promising future. By the end of the 1470s, Florence had eighty-four woodworking studios, fifty-four marble and stone workshops, and forty-four gold- and silversmith businesses. What's interesting about the fifteenth-century Florentine craftsmen compared with the artisans of today is that many of them led double lives. Famous artists whom we normally associate with the "fine arts" and whose paintings and sculptures fill up the Uffizi Gallery and the Pitti Palace moonlighted as furniture and dinnerware decorators. Art history scholars are always baffled when they read that Filippino Lippi and Botticelli painted wedding scenes on wooden hope chests, that Donatello carved out coats of arms for the "new" nobility, that Verrocchio sculpted terra-cotta figurines, that Luca della Robbia fired wall tiles for palazzo kitchens.

The Donatellos and Verrocchios of the fifteenth century may have produced masterpieces for churches, private chapels, and palazzos, but their output and style was always dictated by the tastes of the merchant-patron. This restraint on his talents caused the artist/ craftsman of this period to develop business skills: how to charm, how to haggle, how to persuade, and how to sell. He learned what people wanted, and with these skills he eventually learned that he could make it on his own without the support of one steady patron. This was a turning point in art history and a change that marked the difference between medieval and Renaissance art because as soon as the artist discovered that he could become financially independent, he was in a position to express his own tastes and ideas. By the time the sixteenth century rolled in, the successful professional artist was a combination businessman, celebrity, and spokesman for the times. This era saw some of the great masters, such as Michelangelo and Cellini, still enjoying patronage, but on a wider, more varied scale, and now also enjoying new prestige and social mobility. The crafts industry continued to flourish, but with a more limited focus on producing beautiful, functional objects that would appeal to the general populace and enhance domestic environments.

Via dei Vellutini is a small side street no more than 100 yards in length. Begin strolling down it, but be sure to stop at the end of the street before walking into the open square. On your right are two woodworking studios that have housed Florentine furniture businesses for well over four hundred years. If you're walking in the morning or the late afternoon, you'll be able to look into the open doors of the workshops and watch carpenters lathing ridges into chair legs, gluing a reproduction eighteenth-century table, or sanding down the frame of a Cinquecento mirror.

Stop at the end of via dei Vellutini. To your right at no. 5/r is a large, slightly battered wooden door with a handwritten sign tacked onto it that reads: "*Aperto/ Open.*" If the door is closed, give it a slight push and walk inside a woodworking studio that's a baroque fantasy of carved chairs and tables, wall plaques engraved with fruits and flowers, thin strips of moldings etched with scallops, Corinthian, Doric, and Ionic columns, hanging wrought-iron chandeliers, grotesque masks, life-size cupids, geese, swans, sullen Madonnas, and imitation Renaissance marble birdbaths. Bertolino, the proprietor of this one-of-a-kind studio, is happy to see visitors wandering around his eclectic array of architectural and sculptural pieces, and he's fond of telling guests that his workshop is "just like Verrocchio's from the Quattrocento days." Forty artisans carve, chisel, mold, weld, and sketch design patterns in this sprawling complex of workrooms. Bertolino's craftsmen are in the business of reproducing antiques and art objects. Clients from all over the world mail in photographs of eighteenth-century English water pitchers, statuettes from a grandmother's attic, and fireplace mantels from baronial châteaux in the French countryside, and ask for reproductions. With an abundance of imagination, years of experience, and a dash of guesswork, Bertolino's ingenious crew is able to duplicate almost any sculptural form from bits of wood, sheets of iron, or blocks of Carrara marble. Stroll around the smaller rooms behind the skylit showroom. In back of and to the left of this large room is the drafting studio. Faded photographs and charcoal sketches are pinned to easels, and artists are busy cre-

Bertolino's workshop (via dei Vellutini)

ating the plans from which the craftsmen will work.

Bertolino's biggest customers these days are affluent Arabs who want to decorate newly acquired mansions in Beverly Hills with a motif somewhere between Taj Mahal and Palace of Versailles. On an ordinary business day in the large showroom an assemblage of wood-carvers was putting the finishing touches on the latticework of wall paneling personally commissioned by the royal family of Saudi Arabia. Some of the artworks in this room are unclaimed or unpaid for. If something catches your eye or you're interested in doing some commissioning yourself, don't be shy about walking over to the clerical offices located between the showroom and the drafting room.

The open square in front of Bertolino's workshop is temporarily nameless. One local resident provided the puzzling information that the square was once called Piazza della Passero ("Piazza of the Sparrow"), but a neighborhood committee recently voted to change the name. No alternative has as yet been found acceptable.

Our walk continues along via Toscanella. If you are facing the square with your back to the door of the workshop, turn to your right and walk past the side-walk trattoria on the corner (unless you are hungry). The small, slightly meandering street directly in front of you is via Toscanella, another busy enclave for woodworking artisans, and the birthplace of Giovanni Boccaccio, the fourteenth-century author of some of the bawdiest tales in Italian literature.

Turn left on via Toscanella. Walk a few feet down this street and pause at the intersection of via dello Sprone. This cross-street was the musical-instrument manufacturing center of medieval Florence. The crafts-men of this street specialized in trumpets, bugles, and horns that were used for the popular street festivals and church ceremonies of the day.

Continue walking down via Toscanella. More furni-ture studios and a blacksmith's shop are lodged in the centuries-old structures along the right side of the street. At the end of this narrow passage on the left is the backyard wall of Casa Sorbi, one last medieval tower that we'll stop in front of in a moment.

The walk will resume with a left turn at this corner, but first you may want to take a short detour: turn right at this intersection and make your way cautiously down the threadlike sidewalk on the right side of Borgo San Jacopo. (The motorcycle and automobile traffic can whiz treacherously close to your elbows during the rush hours.) About a dozen yards away from the intersection is the very modern apartment-building entrance marked no. 11. Walk through the front door and into the original courtyard of what once was a thirteenth-century palace. All four walls and the roof of the palace were blasted to rubble by the German attack on Florence in the last World War. The medieval Gothic capitals that you see were res-cued before the bombing, and hidden away for several years. After the war the new apartment building was constructed around the ancient courtyard. The capitals were retrieved, ceremoniously placed back on stone columns, and their seven-hundred-year-old residency in Borgo San Jacopo was resumed.

Seventy-five yards down from this apartment build-ing is the fourteenth-century Ponte Vecchio. Don't wander down there right now—but you may want to read a little about the recent history of the street and the bridge. When the Germans entered Florence in August 1944, the Allied troops were not far behind. With the intention of slowing the enemy advance, the German bombers laid waste to five of the six historical bridges that spanned the Arno. The Ponte Vecchio was spared but only at the expense of the surrounding neighborhoods on either side of the structure. In an effort to discourage access to the bridge, the Germans shelled all buildings that were within 200 meters of both bridgeheads of the Ponte Vecchio. Across the river the old goldsmiths' shops and many thirteenth-century towers were destroyed. On this side of the river, almost half of Borgo San Jacopo was the target. A row of medieval towers that had hugged the river for half a dozen centuries was demolished in a matter of minutes.

Among the casualties never accounted for after that sunny August day were thirty-two priceless Italian masterpieces. American-born Bernard Berenson, unsurpassed connoisseur of Renaissance paintings and international art consultant, had spent a good part of his career cultivating and caring for a collection that was unique in the private-owner world. Berenson was seventy-nine years old and enjoying life at his beloved villa "i Tatti" in the nearby hills of Settignano when the German troops sounded their imminent arrival at the cradle of Renaissance civilization. Consulate officials, aware of his great celebrity and Jewish heritage, immediately granted the scholar a special permit to return to the United States as soon as possible. Berenson flatly refused to leave his paradise overlooking Florence. Finally, after great persuasion from his family and friends, he agreed to move to another nearby villa, but continued to have his laundry sent by bicycle to be cleaned and pressed by a household maid still residing at "i Tatti." As a last precautionary measure Berenson gathered up his art collection and gave it to his secretary's sister to stow away in the basement of her apartment in Borgo San Jacopo. After the bombing raid, the art treasures disappeared along with the towers, palaces, and bridges around the Ponte Vecchio. Berenson survived the perils of war with his usual aplomb. After the armistice, he returned to "i Tatti," dusted off the furniture, and lived out his last fifteen years in style

Sixteenth-century della Robbia altarpiece over the doorway of Casa Sorbi (Borgo San Jacopo 17)

and comfort. Berenson's frequent trips down to Florence were to visit the great art galleries, call on old friends, and raise money to rebuild the ruined Ponte S. Trinità.

One surviving medieval tower with a remarkable piece of artwork built onto its façade is back on the corner where we made our detour.

Return to the intersection of via Toscanella and Borgo San Jacopo. Stand in front of but across the street from no. 17, which is undergoing renovation. This is Casa Sorbi, once the home to nineteenth-century art lover Giuseppe Sorbi, who, in a mood of lavish eccentricity, hung up this sixteenth-century della Robbia altarpiece of the Annunciation over his doorway in 1830. Both Andrea and Giovanni della Robbia may have worked on this piece, but it's probable that Giovanni had a larger hand in the outcome; the figures are lively and the multicolored robes and elaborate fruit garlands around the frame are more typical of Giovanni's fondness for ornamental effect. Behind the figures of the Madonna and S. Gabriel is an open-air loggia with the distinctive della Robbia turquoise-colored glaze of the background sky.

The final lap of our walk continues down Borgo San Jacopo in the direction of Ponte S. Trinità. On your right is the thirteenth-century Church of San Jacopo Soprarno, one of the twelve oldest churches in Florence. The interior was remodeled in the eighteenth century.

Next door are five small fifteenth-century shops that were once part of the church's monastery. Notice the "S.J.A." emblems above the windows. Some Florentines believe that the one-room shops were once chapels, and that only later when the church needed additional revenue were they rented out to artisans. Look inside the frame shop and you'll see an old workman's ledge built in under the window facing the street. This arrangement was made so that the craftsman could catch the greatest amount of natural light during his long hours in the shop.

Across the street is a wide selection of restaurants. Near Casa Sorbi is Trattoria Mama Gina (no. 37/r), whose prices are a bit higher than modest. At no. 57/r is Trattoria Cammillo, with a large choice of native Tuscan dishes. Again, the meals are priced slightly above modest. The surroundings are pleasant and not overbearingly charming and rustic.

Our last stopping-off point is at the end of Borgo San Jacopo. On the left side of the street, facing out toward the Piazza dei Frescobaldi, is a whimsical baroque wall fountain with a steady stream of water gushing from the mouth of a whiskered sea monster. Scholars generally attribute this piece of urban artwork to the leading architect of Florence in the second half of the sixteenth century, Bernardo Buontalenti.

Throughout that century notable changes in city living and artistic attitudes were taking place. More and more foreign visitors were heading for Florence to do business and practice diplomacy. The Renaissance city assumed a new air of cosmopolitanism, and Florence became appearance-conscious. The sixteenth century was also a time when outdoor plays, pageants, parades, and jousting tournaments in public squares became a passionate pastime for both the wealthy and the working classes. The streets, piazzas, bridges, and the Arno became part of a vast stage for urban entertainment of all kinds. Finally, with a renewed interest in the literature and art of the past, Florentines became infatuated with every aspect of Greek and Roman culture. Sixteenth-century artists were tired of painting the solemn, awesome religious themes, and they took to creating garden statues, gargoyles, pavilions, and fountains in pagan motifs of sea monsters, river gods, dolphins, lions, and fire-breathing dragons, all of which came tumbling out of classical mythology. With this change of tide toward the secular, painting lost its status as foremost in the hearts of many artists. Designing imaginative sculptures and bizarre, chimerical buildings was far more appealing.

The appreciation of painting by the general public was also problematic. Most of the great works were either ensconced on the high walls or in dark chapels of churches, or hidden away in the private halls of merchant princes. Also, a viewer experienced painting and sculpture in very different ways. Paintings are flat and if displayed at a distance create a strong sense of detachment between viewer and artwork. The viewer studies a painting from one vantage point, one angle. The aesthetic experience is remote, stationary, similar to worship. Outdoor sculptural figures, such as the assemblage in the Piazza della Signoria and Michelangelo's *David*, which originally resided there, became popular in the sixteenth century for the same reasons that the colorful pageants and parades stirred up the crowds. Statues of satyric Greek gods and outrageously endowed sea creatures provided an aura of excitement, amusement, and spontaneity. Marble figures are evocative in a way that paintings are not. A viewer can walk all around a sculpture, look closely at supple muscles, arched backs, and expressive hands, and really feel texture and movement in his very fingertips. Sculptors of this late Renaissance era were fully aware of this sensual effect, and they played it to the fullest.

Buontalenti was a master of production and design; he comes close to Leonardo da Vinci in filling the role of "Renaissance Man." When he wasn't busy working as the public architect, engineer, and superintendent of the Florence waterworks, Buontalenti was designing war machines, water mills, theater props, and costumes, and choreographing water ballets and orchestrating elaborate fireworks displays. He was also

a pioneer in the field of airconditioning and ice cream refrigeration. The architect cleverly constructed a stone annex around part of his house, loaded up the space with chunks of ice and barrels of ice cream, and drilled a few holes through the other walls to allow the cool air to drift into the adjacent rooms.

One of the most startling structures in all of Florence is Buontalenti's famous *Grotto* in the Boboli Gardens behind the left wing of the Pitti Palace. There you'll find a mausoleumlike building guarded by statues of Apollo and Ceres, embellished with columns and capitals of the Doric order, and frosted with hundreds of crusty, stone-carved stalactites dripping from the arched doorway and rooftop.

The building of baroque fountains as fanciful urban art was a natural response to the playful but aesthetic-minded mood of Florence at the end of the sixteenth century. The fountains beautified the city, and the sportive gods and monsters appealed to the Florentine imagination. The fascination with the classical world was also gratified: the sculptural characters from the sea-loving Greek world were perfect centerpieces for the small ponds and fountains that were sprucing up the streets, piazzas, and parks.

The baroque fountain in front of us at the corner of Borgo San Jacopo combines all the pleasurable ideas and romantic associations that the Renaissance Florentines delighted in thinking of as they rolled by in their horse-drawn carriages to a palazzo in via Maggio or as they lazily filled a jug of drinking water for a quiet midday meal.

One last reminder of the Florentine love of pleasure and romance is the small wooden veranda above the fountain that extends from the corner building. The shopkeeper across the street in the leather goods store is a faithful believer in the story that this is where Beatrice would sit knitting and anxiously awaiting the appearance of her beloved Dante. The exact spot in Florence where the legendary couple used to rendezvous is about as dubious as where George Washington

Sixteenth-century baroque wall fountain attributed to Buontalenti (corner of Borgo San Jacopo and via dello Sprone)

spent his nights in the American colonies. Not only is the evidence for this tale scanty but there's also a historical anachronism involved. Beatrice and Dante were lovers in the thirteenth century, and this balcony and the building from which it hangs appear to be of a later date. When told of this discrepancy, the shopkeeper only smiled and replied: "Well, what's a little stretch of the imagination as long as people come by and stop in front of my store?"

Restaurants and Shops

Restaurants

The following restaurants are located on or near the walks in this book. They're popular, even beloved eating establishments in Florence. Telephone numbers are included as reservations are recommended but not always necessary. Don't overlook the many trattorias that are mentioned along the walks; they may never enter the annals of culinary fame but their family-style cooking and friendly service may prove more memorable than many of the more elaborately organized restaurants.

Walk 1

Nella, via delle Terme 19/r, tel. 17.7.81. Simple but carefully prepared Tuscan dishes; restaurant fills up quickly especially for afternoon "dinner." Moderate.

Al lume di candela, via delle Terme 23/r, tel. 294.566. Cosmopolitan clientele and staff; giant shrimp and lobster tails are recommended if you want a break from Florentine steak. Expensive.

Da i Cinque Amici, via de' Cimatori 30/r, tel. 296.672. An unassuming spot for lunch, and near the center of everything. Moderate.

Da Pennello, via Dante Alighieri 4/r, tel. 294.848. A favorite restaurant with Florentine business people; good service. Moderate.

Antico Barile, via dei Cerchi 40/r, tel. 23.1.42. Cheerful and casual; children are enthusiastically welcomed. Moderate.

Ottorino, via Santa Elisabetta 6/r, tel. 218.747. Out-of-the-way location and little discovered by visitors. Moderate.

Walk 2

Le Cantine, via de' Pucci 4/r, tel. 298.879. Tuscan dishes well prepared but not overly imaginative; staff is friendly and English-speaking. Moderate.

Trattoria da Cosimo, via dell'Oriuolo 16/r and Borgo Pinti 4/r, tel. 213.401. Dining rooms are filled with original artwork, and antique accessories lend an almost-Bohemian air to this trattoria. Moderate.

Leo in Santa Croce, via Torta 7/r, tel. 270.829. Long-standing favorite of neighborhood Florentines. Moderate.

Il Fagiano, via de' Neri 57/r, tel. 287.876. Try any game or fowl dishes here; wine selection is impeccable. Expensive.

Walk 3

Mario, via Rosina; northeast corner of Piazza del Mercato Centrale. Boisterous eating crowd at lunch; food is simple but ample; students, merchants, and business people-in-the-know come here to eat and mingle; reservations are not what this small restaurant is about, but come early for lunch. Budget but good.

Trattoria Sostanza, via del Porcellana 25/r, tel. 212.691. An understated "in" spot for international celebrities, but everyone is treated like a celebrity by the incomparable staff. (See p. 140–41.) Expensive.

Al Girarrosto, Piazza Santa Maria Novella 9–10/r, tel. 275.387. Classic Tuscan dishes; upper-crust clientele who know how to wine and dine; if your pocketbook can survive, don't leave Florence without one meal here. Expensive.

Walk 4

Mama Gina, Borgo San Lorenzo 37/r, tel. 296.009. Popular with younger Florentines who are in the arts but not struggling. Moderate.

Cammillo, Borgo San Lorenzo 57/r, tel. 212.427. An unpretentious trattoria; much of the clientele and staff seem to know one another and are friendly to new faces. Moderate.

Off Your Route but Well Worth Trying

Cibreo, via de' Macci 118/4, tel. 677.394. The owner/manager comes to your table to describe (in Italian) the offerings for each course. Superb food. Expensive.

Maremma, via Verdi 16/4, tel. 244.615. A very good, moderately priced restaurant.

La Beppa, via dell'Erta Canina 6/r, tel. 296.390. To savor the eating experience, plan a leisurely fifteen-minute stroll across Ponte alle Grazie, through via San Niccolò, under the fourteenth-century gate, and turn right onto via dell'Erta Canina; this is a Florentine family neighborhood, and when you arrive at La Beppa and take a table in the garden, you'll feel like you're at a villa party. Call ahead for dinner reservations. Expensive.

La Loggia, Piazzale Michelangiolo 1, tel. 287.032. The food is good but the view is the attraction here. Expensive.

Wine Bars and Wine Restaurants

Chianti Così, via de' Cimatori 38/r (Walk 1, page 66).

Vini, volta San Pier Maggiore 6/r (Walk 2, pages 87–89).

Fiaschetteria Niccolini, via de' Neri 17/r (Walk 2, page 103).

Fiaschetteria Il Latini, via Palchetti 6/r (Walk 3, page 137), tel. 270.916. On the ground floor of Palazzo Rucellai.

Shops

Zanobetti, via Calimala 3, tel. 21.06.46 and 29.50.90. Housed in the thirteenth-century Palace of the Wool Guild, this emporium is known for its high-quality sportswear and accessories; walk in even if you're "just looking."

Richard-Ginori, via Rondinelli 7. Porcelain and china; with a branch on New York's Fifth Avenue, this Florentine business is well suited to setting some of the best tables in the world; ex-President Gerald Ford's daughter, Susan, chose her matrimonial dinnerware here; operatic star Anna Moffo, Luciana Pignatelli, and Johnny Carson also do their china shopping at Ginori's.

Gucci, via dei Tornabuoni 73. The last word in leather bags.

Ferragamo, via dei Tornabuoni 2. Scarves, linen dresses, and pumps that complement "the Gucci look."

Cuoieria, Piazza Santa Elisabetta 8/r; Leather craftsman Pierre Cusseau works right in the front window of this pleasant shop filled with moderately priced handbags, belts, and attaché cases designed with a rugged, hand-worked style.

I Maschereri, Borgo Pinti 18/r, tel. 265.147. Papier-mâché and leather theater masks adapted from sixteenth-century commedia dell'arte characters; the price range is from about $25 to $45.

Farmacia di S. Maria Novella, via della Scala 16. Once the seventeenth-century pharmacy of the Dominican friars, this business has been owned and operated by the Stephani family for the last hundred years; soaps, rose water, rice powder, perfumes, and potpourris are sold here and at Henri Bendel's in New York.

Il Papiro, via Cavour 55/r; Hand-dyed stationery, book bindings, cards, and photo albums; ask to be shown into the back-room studio where craftsmen stain individual sheets of paper with an herbal dying technique from the seventeenth-century.

The following are bookstores:

Seeber, via dei Tornabuoni 70/r. Well stocked; many of the clerks speak English.

Porcellino, Piazza del Mercato Nuovo 6–8/r. Plenty of English paperbacks; variety of calendars with modern and eighteenth-century scenes of Florence.

Salimbeni, via Matteo Palmieri 6/r. The largest selection of art and architecture books in Florence.

Bruno Baccani, via Porta Rossa 99/r. Looking for a *Time*, *Newsweek*, or *Cosmopolitan*? Almost every major American magazine is here.

Index

Index

Index

Index

Index